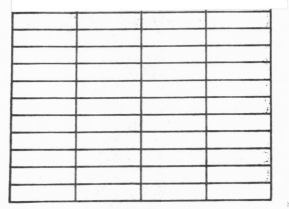

Current Issues in Leisure Services

Looking Ahead in a Time of Transition

Edited by
Joseph J. Bannon

PRACTICAL MANAGEMENT SERIES
Barbara H. Moore, Editor

Current Issues in Leisure Services
Capital Financing Strategies for Local Governments
Creative Personnel Practices
The Entrepreneur in Local Government
Human Services on a Limited Budget
Long-Term Financial Planning
Managing New Technologies
Microcomputers in Local Government
Police Management Today
Practical Financial Management
Productivity Improvement Techniques
Risk Management Today
Shaping the Local Economy
Successful Negotiating in Local Government
Telecommunications for Local Government

 # 156 30314

58408
GV
181.5
C87
1987

The Practical Management Series is devoted to the
presentation of information and ideas from diverse
sources. The views expressed in this book are those of
the contributors and are not necessarily those of the
International City Management Association.

Library of Congress Cataloging in Publication Data

Main entry under title:
Current issues in leisure services.
    (Practical management series)
    Bibliography: p.
    1. Recreation—Management.   2. Parks—Management.
3. Leisure industry—Management.   I. Bannon, Joseph J.
II. International City Management Association.
III. Series.
BV181.5.C87   1987   790′.068   87-2792
ISBN 0-87326-050-3

Printed in the United States of America
929190898887
54321

Foreword

Today's leisure services managers know that their jobs are more complex—and more rewarding—than ever before. They face a number of challenges, including limited financial resources, shifting demographic patterns, and changing public expectations. *Current Issues in Leisure Services* looks at some of the most difficult and controversial issues in leisure services management and offers practical, innovative approaches to dealing with them.

The provision of equitable, responsive, high-quality programs and services is the goal of every leisure services agency, but a rapidly changing environment and daily pressures may make it difficult to keep that goal in sight. *Current Issues in Leisure Services* begins with the basics of long-term program planning, then explores the careful evaluation that is planning's necessary complement. Because its human resources are any agency's most valuable resource, *Current Issues in Leisure Services* includes a section on selecting and evaluating personnel and on encouraging productivity. Next it considers financial management, which, in an era of fiscal constraint, is crucial to maintaining programs and services. Risk management, another problematic aspect of management, is analyzed both as an economic and legal phenomenon and as a practical matter that can be approached through practical means. Finally, *Current Issues in Leisure Services* looks at the future—at the special skills, competencies, and attitudes that will help leisure services managers meet the challenge of rapid social and technological change.

We are grateful to Joseph J. Bannon, Professor of Leisure Studies at the University of Illinois at Urbana-Champaign, for organizing and compiling the volume. Special thanks are extended to James Busser and Rodney Buhr for their assistance in an extensive literature search and manuscript review. We also appreciate the cooperation of the organizations and individuals who granted ICMA permission to reprint their materials. Thanks also go to David S. Arnold, who helped plan the entire Practical Management Series.

William H. Hansell, Jr.
Executive Director
International City
Management Association

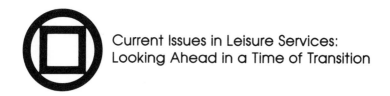 Current Issues in Leisure Services:
Looking Ahead in a Time of Transition

The International City Management Association is the professional and educational organization for chief appointed management executives in local government. The purposes of ICMA are to enhance the quality of local government and to nurture and assist professional local government administrators in the United States and other countries. In furtherance of its mission, ICMA develops and disseminates new approaches to management through training programs, information services, and publications.

Managers, carrying a wide range of titles, serve cities, towns, counties, and councils of governments in all parts of the United States and Canada. These managers serve at the direction of elected councils and governing boards. ICMA serves these managers and local governments through many programs that aim at improving the manager's professional competence and strengthening the quality of all local governments.

The International City Management Association was founded in 1914; adopted its City Management Code of Ethics in 1924; and established its Institute for Training in Municipal Administration in 1934. The Institute, in turn, provided the basis for the Municipal Management Series, generally termed the "ICMA Green Books."

ICMA's interests and activities include public management education; standards of ethics for members; the *Municipal Year Book* and other data services; urban research; and newsletters, a monthly magazine, *Public Management,* and other publications. ICMA's efforts for the improvement of local government management—as represented by this book—are offered for all local governments and educational institutions.

About the Editor and Authors

Joseph J. Bannon is Professor of Leisure Studies and former head of the Department of Leisure Studies at the University of Illinois at Urbana-Champaign. Before joining the faculty at the University of Illinois, he served as General Superintendent of Recreation for the Topeka Recreation Commission and as Director of Recreation for the Leonia Recreation Commission. He is a member of the Academy of Leisure Science and the Academy of Park and Recreation Administration. Dr. Bannon holds a B.S. degree from Ithaca College and an M.S. and Ph.D. from the University of Illinois.

Joseph J. Bannon, Jr., Associate, Peterson, Ross, Schloerb, and Seidel, Chicago, Illinois.

Lauren B. Bannon, Director of Sponsorship, Chicago Area Runners' Association.

Frank Benest, Director of Parks and Recreation, Colton, California.

Kenneth W. Brooks, Vice President, Johnson, Romanowitz, architects, Lexington, Kentucky.

Jerry D. Burnam, Assistant Dean of the College of Applied Life Studies, University of Illinois, Urbana-Champaign.

James Busser, Lecturer in the Department of Leisure Studies, University of Illinois, Urbana-Champaign.

Monty L. Christiansen, Associate Professor, Department of Recreation and Parks, The Pennsylvania State University.

John L. Crompton, Professor, Department of Recreation and Parks, Texas A & M University.

Michael Farley, Senior Management Analyst, Bureau of Parks and Recreation, Portland, Oregon.

Jack Foley, Assistant Professor, Department of Leisure Studies, California State University, Northridge.

Seymour M. Gold, Professor of Environmental Planning, Division of Environmental Planning and Management, University of California, Davis.

David Gray, President, David Gray and Associates, Long Beach, California.

Daniel G. Hobbs, Assistant City Manager, Rockville, Maryland.

Christine Z. Howe, Associate Professor, Department of Recreation and Leisure Studies, University of Georgia.

Sharon L. Hunt, Associate Professor, Department of Recreation and Leisure Studies, University of Kentucky.

William R. McKinney, Assistant Professor, Department of Leisure Studies, University of Illinois, Urbana-Champaign.

J. Robert Rossman, Chairman of the Division of Health, Physical Education, and Leisure Studies, North Texas University.

H. Douglas Sessoms, Chairman and Professor of Recreation, University of North Carolina, Chapel Hill.

Ted Tedrick, Assistant Professor, Department of Leisure Studies, State University of New York, Brockport.

J. P. Tindell, Recreation Planner, City of San Jose, California.

James R. Waters, former Associate Professor, Department of Recreation and Leisure Studies, University of Georgia.

George Welton, Professor, Department of Recreation and Leisure Studies, California State University, Northridge.

Contents

Introduction

Joseph J. Bannon and James A. Busser

Managing in the decade ahead is of primary concern to recreation
and park professionals. The articles in this volume examine the issues that are paramount to the effective and efficient delivery of
leisure services—now and in the foreseeable future. Five major
themes cover the most important issues facing today's leisure service professionals: planning and evaluation, personnel and productivity, budgeting and finance, risk management, and the future.

The importance of planning stems from current crises. First,
we are living in an era of widespread and continuing threats to environmental and ecological resources. Second, there is growing concern among both leisure service professionals and their clients
about social, ethical, financial, and professional accountability.
Since the 1960s, the profession has been under some criticism for
failing to distribute services equitably. While equity in the delivery
of services may be a philosophical tenet in the field, it needs to be
transferred to practice. As budgetary constraints increase, the public will give increasing attention to the spectrum of services delivered to constituent groups. Only through careful and responsive
planning and evaluation can leisure service professionals meet both
environmental and social needs.

Management of employee relations is a major challenge facing
both public and private organizations. In addition to constituent or
consumer satisfaction, leisure service managers must consider employee satisfaction. Job satisfaction has been linked to decreases in
turnover, absenteeism, and grievances, as well as to increases in the
speed at which employees learn new tasks. To create a rewarding
work environment, managers need to understand that they are hiring whole people who bring their values, aspirations, and problems—as well as their skills—to work. Employees expect more from

their jobs than just a paycheck; managers who understand and respect emerging employee demands for participation and responsibility will be best able to make use of the full range of staff resources.

Well-designed selection and evaluation practices are central to good personnel management. The literature on evaluation has grown steadily during the past twenty years, offering managers sound and systematic programs for appraising individual as well as organizational performance. Leisure service managers need no longer rely on intuition or personal judgment, which are arbitrary assessments that can be easily challenged, legally and otherwise.

Financial and risk management are and will continue to be major concerns for all administrators of leisure services. Reduction of appropriations for almost every social service has become commonplace, and leisure services, often considered a low priority by local governments, have been particularly hard hit by budget reductions. Twenty-seven states currently limit the taxing powers of state government. At the same time, federal financial retrenchment has put an increased burden on state legislatures, which have, in turn, passed this burden on to the local level.

The current fiscal climate has encouraged a more entrepreneurial style of leisure service management, evidenced by widespread use of fees and charges to support programs that may at one time have been offered "free." Although fees and charges will be used by most leisure service organizations in the coming decade, administrators must ensure that the policies governing those charges are based on ethical and equitable principles.

Leisure service management is at a crossroads; change is the only certainty. The most important task for leisure service professionals is to ensure that their organizations move into the coming decade thoughtfully, making considered and deliberate choices. New leadership skills and styles are emerging; leisure service managers may find that they work more *with* than *for* the community; many will have to find new ways to respond to traditional social needs.

This volume addresses the most pressing issues currently facing leisure service professionals. Although it cannot possibly be all-inclusive, it covers topics that are central to increasing the effectiveness and improving the quality of services delivered to the public we serve.

PART 1

Planning and Evaluating Leisure Services

A Human Service Approach to Recreation Planning

Seymour M. Gold

The task of translating human needs and leisure behavior into space and services requires an understanding of the process and products of recreation planning. It also requires an understanding of the nature of recreation planning and selected concepts or principles that can be used to solve problems or realize potentials at both the systems and site-planning scales.

A human service approach to recreation planning is needed and possible. It is the most cost-effective way to cope with the changing nature of many cities and suburbs. This approach requires

1. The integration of recreation planning with other types of functional planning
2. A broader definition of recreation space and services
3. Active citizen involvement in the planning process.

Nature of recreation planning

Recreation planning is a process that relates the leisure time of people to space. The process results in products (plans, studies, information) that condition the public policy and private initiatives used to provide leisure opportunities. In the broadest sense, recreation planning is concerned with human development and the stewardship of land because it helps people relate to their environment and to each other. In a narrow sense, recreation planning is most concerned with the variables of leisure behavior and open space (Gold 1980:5).

Recreation planning develops alternatives for public and pri-

From the *Journal of Park and Recreation Administration* 1, no. 1 (January 1983). Reprinted with permission from the Academy of Park and Recreation Administration.

vate sector policy decisions. It should be representative of what people want, imaginative in projecting what might be, and realistic in recognizing what is possible. It is based on the following ideas:

1. Cities are for people.
2. Change, complexity, and compromise are the essence of cities.
3. Planning is a means of anticipating or reacting to change.

Scope and context of recreation planning

The scope and context of recreation planning has paralleled the development of cities and the park and recreation movement. The emerging emphasis of recreation planning blends environmental design, social science, and public administration to provide leisure opportunities that are part of a human service and environmental management system. Both public and private spaces and services are included in a system of opportunities integrated at the neighborhood and metropolitan scales.

Emerging in many communities is an emphasis on human development; environmental management; systems planning; self-generated design and management; recycling developed land into open space; noncompetitive, self-programmed activities; creative play areas; and integration of the arts, culture, senior citizens, day care, and adult education programs with parks and recreation.

Special programs for the mentally retarded and physically handicapped are considered the responsibility of park and recreation departments. Community gardens, day-care centers, skateboard parks, and fitness programs are activities sponsored by park and recreation agencies. A new generation of spaces is supplementing existing resources in cities, including roof-tops, cemeteries, pneumatic structures, air rights over parking lots, and recycled obsolete buildings converted to public or private recreation uses.

Previous distinctions between indoor and outdoor spaces and public and private opportunities are fading, to be replaced by a broader view of recreation planning that integrates spaces and services. The traditional park or recreation department is becoming part of new agencies with broader missions, e.g., human services, community development, or environmental planning and management.

Recreation planning today requires more sensitive and sophisticated methods than the application of arbitrary standards and conventional wisdom of the past. New demands for citizen participation in the planning and design process, environmental and social impact assessment, the necessity for cost-effective public investments, and the requirements of special populations will make the traditional emphasis of recreation planning seem romantic. These demands call for rethinking the objectives and methods of recreation planning.

Human service approach

The use of leisure time has important implications for community development, resource conservation, and the quality of human existence. These implications mean planners and designers must evaluate the consequences of what they do, asking whether their activities are helping to make people and communities better. A *humanistic* approach to professional practice suggests that park and recreation agencies can

1. Emphasize human development, social welfare, and community integration. Services should be defined in terms of human experiences rather than in terms of activities, programs, and buildings.
2. Provide for the needs of special populations and integrate their efforts with those of other social services.
3. Broaden their philosophy of service to include environmental beautification, public health, energy conservation, and a concern for all aspects of the living environment.
4. Seek a common ground with environmental and consumer groups that are also concerned with improving community life and environment.
5. Plan with, instead of for, people and be held accountable for their actions (Gold 1980:41).

Planning principles   Regardless of the size or character of a community, the following principles of recreation planning should be considered basic to the success of any planning effort and can be used to monitor the quality of the planning process:

1. All people should have access to activities and facilities, regardless of interest, age, sex, income, cultural background, housing environment, or handicap.
2. Public recreation should be coordinated with other community recreation opportunities to avoid duplication and encourage innovation.
3. Public recreation should be integrated with other public services, such as education, health, and transportation.
4. Facilities should be adaptable to rapidly changing and special populations.
5. Citizens should be involved in the planning process throughout all stages.
6. Facilities should make the most efficient use of land; should be designed and managed to provide for the convenience, health, safety, and pleasure of intended users; and should represent positive examples of design, energy use, and a concern for people and the environment.

Design strategies   At the project level, there are some design strategies that can be incorporated into a human service approach to planning.

Most people do not necessarily share a designer's values. They care more about social than physical factors. Their use of the space depends more on who is there than on what is there.

Citizens involved in the design process will contribute information vital to the designer's success. They can communicate their activity preferences and social needs if they are actively involved in the design process.

People learn the benefits of self-determination by involvement in the design process. If denied this opportunity, they may oppose any proposal because it did not respect their right to be involved.

The application of social factors to the design of spaces results in successful spaces that acknowledge territoriality, status, conflict, cooperation, comfort, class, and life cycle, which are important in urban parks.

People involved in the design process like the results better than those who are not involved. They will use and respect the space in proportion to their identity with it.

The planning process

Planning is a continuous and incremental process of developing guidelines for urban development. The concept of development includes preservation or renewal of spaces and services. Recreation planning is a systematic way to anticipate, cause, or monitor change related to the provision of public and private leisure opportunities. The planning process should be

1. *Evolutionary instead of revolutionary.* Radical changes may be necessary in many instances, but they will have a much greater chance of public acceptance if proposed in an incremental or demonstration program.
2. *Pluralistic instead of authoritarian.* The right choice is a matter of value, not fact, and is based on a consideration of several alternatives from individuals or groups with different objectives.
3. *Objective instead of subjective.* The criteria or methodology used to describe alternatives should be based on facts, even though the final decision may be based on subjective values.
4. *Realistic instead of politically naive.* Parks and recreation should develop a constituency to compete on its own merits in the decision-making or budget process.
5. *Humanistic instead of bureaucratic.* The approach to develop-

ing a plan, design, or service should serve people instead of the public agency responsible for providing leisure opportunities or preparing the plan.

The planning process has five stages: (1) survey and analysis, (2) goal formulation, (3) development of alternatives, (4) implementation, and (5) review and revision.

Although these stages are common to most planning or design efforts, there is considerable difference in the approach, concepts, and methods used to apply the planning process at both the systems and site-planning levels.

Traditional view   According to the traditional view, planning is a static and linear process that follows a series of logical and consecutive steps. Planners begin with the definition of a problem and end with recommendations to solve the problem. The emphasis is on the output, or product, instead of on the input and process. The primary concern is with the *what* and *how* of planning, rather than with *who* participates and *why*. The means often become ends. Implementing the plan becomes the objective instead of the way to achieve an objective.

The traditional planning process attempts to reduce complexity, using arbitrary guidelines or standards to produce uniform spaces or services. Professionals superimpose their values on the process. Citizens are asked to participate in a token way by reviewing plans or proposals prepared by experts. Everything is neatly organized and predictable in terms of timing, responsibility, and outcome. The end product of this process is a two-dimensional physical plan that is relatively inflexible, uniform, and unrepresentative of community values and needs.

New view   The new view of planning sees the process as dynamic and incremental. It begins with the values, behavior, or priorities of many people and accommodates these through political compromise. The emphasis is on input and process. Change, controversy, compromise, and involvement at all stages of the planning process are expected. Ends are used to justify the means. Achieving these ends is more important than the plan and the methods used to prepare it.

The new view attempts to encourage diversity, using criteria that are sensitive to the particular needs of a special population or planning area. The objective is to provide effective spaces or services. Professionals act as resource persons to translate human values into alternatives that people, or their representatives, can consider. Citizen participation is essential and taken seriously at every step in this process. The outcome of the process is not predictable, and the sequence of events may not flow smoothly or in any preconceived pattern. The end product is a set of policies, priorities, or criteria that are relatively flexible, diverse, and representative of community values and needs.

Ingredients of the planning process   Some important criteria and ingredients condition the scope, direction, and products of the planning process. A serious consideration of these items at the beginning of a planning effort should increase its effectiveness.

Performance criteria   Performance criteria outline what should be expected of the planning process. The following criteria can be used to give planners, decision makers, and citizens some guidelines for evaluating both the products and the process of recreation planning.

1. Plans should provide decision makers with internally consistent policy recommendations that can be implemented over time.
2. Plans should assess the probable consequences, costs, and benefits of alternative courses of action.
3. Planning will be effective only to the extent that it is understood and supported by citizens who have been realistically involved in every step of the process.
4. Planning is a continuous process dealing with changing opportunities, problems, and issues that require constant monitoring, evaluation, and feedback through citizen participation.
5. Controversy, compromise, and change are normal dimensions of the planning process that should be acknowledged by all concerned with any planning effort.
6. The planning process and products will be no better than the resources committed to the effort.

Precedent and practice   There is no single formula for the planning process—only precedent and practice. Each situation may require a different approach to fit the needs of the client, planning area, and times. There are no absolutes in the planning process. However, experience indicates that the success or failure of a planning effort can be influenced by these ingredients:

1. *Community support.* Special-interest groups should recognize the need for a plan and be actively involved in the process. The establishment of citizen advisory committees to provide information and serve as a sounding board for political feasibility is essential.
2. *Technical support.* Administrative organization, technical expertise, cooperation, and support of the planning effort by all

public agencies are as important as citizen participation. Fundamental to any planning effort is the establishment of technical advisory committees of professionals to collaborate in the planning process and resolve the biases of different agencies or professional groups.

3. *Work program.* A detailed program to establish the timing and responsibility for each task is essential. The problem, planning area, planning period, and methods of data collection, analysis, or reporting should be established in advance and formally agreed to by all involved in the planning effort.

4. *Data collection.* Systematic data collection and analysis are the foundation of a sound planning program. Alternatives cannot be developed or considered without the facts. The planning process should have a credible data base to provide a context for resolving issues.

5. *Political compromise.* The facts should provide an objective basis for the development of alternatives that can be considered in the decision process, although the ultimate choice may be a matter of value instead of fact.

6. *Developing alternatives.* The development, selection, and testing of alternatives is the most difficult part of the planning process. Achieving consensus on which alternative best reflects the preliminary goals and policies is crucial to the success of any planning effort.

7. *Future perspective.* A bold, imaginative view of the foreseeable future based on the best available facts or interpretation of near-certain trends is essential. The plan must be future-oriented to serve as a guide for decisions.

Park and recreation plans

The park and recreation plan is an expression of a community's objectives, needs, and priorities for leisure space, services, and facilities. It should provide a guide for public policy and private decisions related to the scope, quality, and location of leisure opportunities. The plan should be considered an important element of the comprehensive plan, detailing recreation needs and the implementation program to meet these needs.

The plan should be a long-range, comprehensive, and policy-oriented document that (1) describes alternatives, recommendations, and guidelines for decisions related to the use and preservation of open space for recreation; and (2) makes recommendations on the acquisition, development, and management of both public and private space or facilities.

The plan should describe the present use and non-use of facilities and project future needs with words, graphics, or data that communicate the facts, outline alternatives, and propose new ideas.

The plan should outline what is possible, explain who can best provide these recreation opportunities, and assess the tangible benefits and costs of policy options in a time-phased program.

Although most existing plans have focused on the public sector, outdoor spaces, and organized programs, the trend is toward a balanced emphasis on the public and private sector, indoor and outdoor opportunities, and the integration of space, services, and facilities. Figures 1 and 2 indicate the breadth and scope of a human services approach to recreation planning (Murphy 1977:134).

Characteristics of a plan   The park and recreation plan should emphasize those aspects of land use, circulation, conservation, and community facilities that detail how and where people use their leisure time. Most communities will also have a separate conservation and open space element of the comprehensive plan with a broader

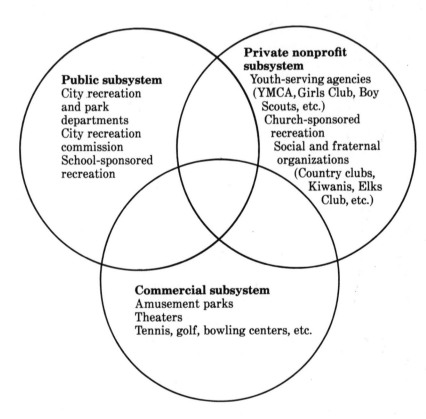

Figure 1. Community recreation system.

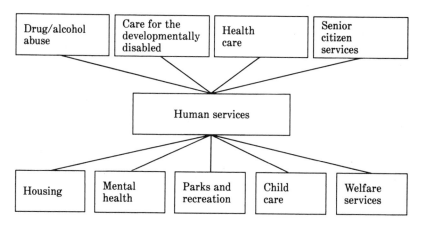

Figure 2. Scope of a human services department.

set of objectives, such as growth management, resource production management, or public safety.

The plan should be

1. Balanced to meet present deficiencies and future needs
2. Oriented to the projected population and economic base of a community
3. In scale with the community's fiscal resources or expected federal and state assistance programs that will be helping to implement the plan.

An effective plan will

1. Identify problems
2. Present relevant information on the social and physical implications of these problems in measurable human terms
3. Include problem-solving alternatives and describe the expected results of each in terms of the environmental and social impact on the planning area
4. Rank or recommend alternatives in terms of economic, social, and political feasibility.

A comprehensive recreation plan should include those places traditionally considered public park and recreation areas, but it can also include facilities such as shopping centers, amusement parks, theaters, restaurants, libraries, museums, airports, farmers' and flea markets, private yacht and sport clubs, community colleges, historic districts, hotel and motel districts, waterfront districts, and pedestrian malls and plazas.

This approach views the entire city as a recreation system instead of as a set of isolated spaces and experiences. It integrates space and services, public and private suppliers, and indoor and out-door facilities where appropriate and possible. It considers any place where people can experience diversity, pleasure, or enrich-ment as a potential leisure resource.

Components and work program   The basic planning task is to inventory, analyze, and project information that relates people (be-havior), time (leisure), and activity (recreation) to space (resources) and a geographic area (planning unit), using criteria or measures (performance standards/social indicators) that are sensitive to the changing physical character, social needs, and political priorities of a community. This information can be used to identify deficiencies by planning unit and population subgroups for specific activities or spaces. It can also be used to establish regional, citywide, and neigh-

---

Introduction
Describe objectives and scope of plan
Define legal authority for federal/state programs
Define agency responsible for preparation of plan
Describe previous and future studies related to plan
State assumptions and qualifications of plan

Existing conditions
Describe regional context of planning area
Describe leisure behavior patterns of population
Describe environmental characteristics of planning area
Describe recreation problems and potentials of planning units
Describe general character of planning units

Recreation resources
Classify resources and opportunities
Inventory existing land, facilities, and programs
Evaluate opportunities by planning unit
Describe potential recreation resources/programs
Evaluate design, access, and public safety

Demand and use patterns
Inventory time budgets of population
Analyze recreation use patterns by demographic groups
Describe user preference/satisfaction
Analyze causes for non-use of existing opportunities
Describe problems of special populations
Assess impact of nonresidents/tourists
Assess impact of fees and charges on demand patterns
Assess impact of access on use of facilities

Figure 3. Components of a work program for a park and recreation plan.

borhood policies. The major heads in Figure 3 list the components of a recreation plan. The items below each head list the individual steps used to prepare each component.

Relationship to comprehensive plan   The comprehensive plan is a general guide to the future character and development of a community. It identifies significant areas to be preserved or changed to achieve social, economic, or environmental goals. The park and recreation plan uses the factual information, policies, standards, design, or management programs that will achieve the leisure objectives of residents and visitors.

The comprehensive plan focuses on the overall relationship of open space and leisure services to land use and the quality of urban life and environment. The park and recreation plan details these

---

Needs analysis
Analyze demand-supply relationships
Develop use concepts, principles, and design criteria
Develop space, development, and program standards
Describe deficiencies by planning unit
Project needs by planning period and planning unit
Describe public/private potentials to accommodate needs

Goals, policies, and alternatives
Describe existing goals, objectives, and policies
Describe desirable goals, objectives, and policies
Analyze alternative ways to achieve desirable goals
Describe the implications of each alternative
Recommend one alternative
Describe social and environmental impact of alternative

Implementation
Describe public/private actions by project/planning unit
Schedule actions by time period, planning unit, responsibility
Estimate benefits and costs of each project or program
Relate costs to general and capital improvement budgets
Describe needed financing
Describe needed new legislation or responsibility
Describe public participation to approve and implement plan
Describe how, when, and who will revise plan

Appendix
Background studies
Data and methodology
Bibliography and sources
Acknowledgments and credits

Figure 3—continued.

relationships and translates them into specific sites to acquire or develop for leisure uses. It also details policies, practices, or criteria related to the design and management of leisure spaces and services.

The comprehensive plan provides the basis for a community's recreation plan and should be completed first. It provides general concepts and goals for the social and physical development of a community. The recreation plan details a community's recreation needs with specific recommendations for land acquisition, facility development, operations, maintenance, and financing that are not normally part of the comprehensive plan. If properly done, both the comprehensive plan and recreation plan will complement each other and satisfy requirements for federal and state assistance.

A human service approach: A constructive alternative
Recreation planning for the 1980s and beyond will require more sensitive and sophisticated methods than the application of arbitrary standards and conventional thinking.

The need to integrate parks and recreation with human service planning is essential in an era of limits. A human service approach to planning offers a constructive alternative with great potential as the critical link to developing a broad political constituency for urban parks and recreation. The option of integrating human and leisure services in many communities is a logical step toward improving the quality of life in urban and suburban America.

Bibliography
Gold, Seymour M. 1979. "Recreation Space, Services and Facilities," in *The Practice of Local Government Planning*, Frank So et al. Washington, D.C.: International City Management Association.

————. 1980. *Recreation Planning and Design.* New York: McGraw-Hill.

Murphy, James F., and Dennis R. Howard. 1977. *Delivery of Community Leisure Services: An Holistic Approach.* Philadelphia: Lea and Febiger.

A Planning Model for Public Recreation Agencies

Sharon L. Hunt and Kenneth W. Brooks

The evolution of planning has paralleled that of society, from a simple preparation to survive the immediate future to a complicated tool employed by organizational leaders. The time is fast approaching when planning will no longer be merely helpful but will be a prerequisite for success (Ewing 1969:3). As Lockyer (1967:1) has stated, "The need for planning has always been present, but the complexity and competitiveness of modern undertakings now require that this need should be met rather than just recognized."

Planning in the United States has progressed somewhat faster in private organizations than in public agencies. To a considerable extent, Zaltman and Duncan (1977:26) attribute this fact to opposition to government planning resulting from equating it with the extension of government in general into private realms. Planning is simply a value-loaded term: it induces a reaction of either sympathetic approval or hostile negation. To those uncomfortable with it, the word conjures up totalitarian states such as the Soviet Union or contemporary China as stereotypes; conversely, others imagine Sweden with full employment, high educational attainment, absences of extreme wealth or poverty, and a highly developed social welfare system. Planning in the latter case is synonymous with good government, economic efficiency, social justice, and political rationality.

Fear of planning

Many recreation agencies would prefer to avoid planning if they could find a substitute means of achieving the same ends. Some of

From the *Journal of Park and Recreation Administration* 1, no. 3 (April 1983). Reprinted with permission from the Academy of Park and Recreation Administration.

the planning-related fears that professionals often reveal are as follows:

1. It is hard to plan (and we might not do a good job).
2. It puts constraints on our actions (if it is not in the plan, we cannot do it).
3. It forces us to make decisions (and that makes us vulnerable).
4. A plan provides a yardstick for critique and evaluation (and we might not measure up).
5. Planning brings direction and organization out of chaos (and removes a very good excuse).
6. Planning brings its own chaos and disruption (when managers resist or choose not to follow the plan) (Reinharth, Shapiro, and Kallman 1981:6).

Chakraborty and David (1981:13) have pointed out that professionals fear the planning process because it thrusts them into complex situations with a great degree of uncertainty, situations with which they often cannot cope. The plan provides information to others within the agency or the community, thus decreasing privacy and exposing errors in forecasting and judgment. It enforces cohesiveness and integration and appears to pose a threat to the independence of top-level administrators. In agencies where the motives and operating principles of superiors are suspect, it would be risky for an administrator to expose himself. Secrecy and minimal involvement are the safest approach, for if there is no documentation, there is no easy way of assessing performance.

Plans versus planning
Although plans are valuable, the planning process itself is more important. A public recreation department gains significant benefits just by moving through the organized, logical, and systematic process of developing a plan. Some of the benefits are immediate; for example, weaknesses, strengths, threats, and opportunities are discovered during the analysis. Even the initial step of defining the purposes and goals of the organization often provides administrators with a much-needed clarification of where the organization is headed.

Planning is a continuing management function; it is never finished. The planning process includes many stages—from developing the planning process to implementing it. Implementation is always followed by feedback: that is, the original premises developed are continually tested against reality, and, as reality changes, the planning process must be reinstituted and the premises reworked. In other words, the plan—the result of the planning process—is dynamic, constantly adapting to changes in the internal and external environment. That is the way it must be in recreational planning, because a static plan would be of no value to a dynamic public recreation agency.

Comprehensive recreation planning model

There is a need today in public recreation for a comprehensive planning model that builds on past planning experiences in other fields and is not so unduly complex that it will not be used by recreation practitioners. Comprehensive recreational planning is meant to be a continuous process which is future-oriented and considers both short- and long-range alternatives. It must also be multidimensional and integrate all facets of recreation with other societal agencies. The involvement and coordination of people are key activities throughout the process.

Processes and products of planning model

Figure 1 graphically presents the process of comprehensive recreational planning by using rectangles to designate processes and circles to designate products of the processes. The model shown is an adaptation of a model first developed in relation to educational organizations (Conrad, Brooks, and Fisher 1973:3-4) and has been applied in a number of educational and governmental settings.

Development of the planning process strategy   The initial phase of planning process strategy development is bipartite: (1) end products of the planning endeavor are clearly identified and stated, and (2) detailed resources—personnel, finances, and time needed to complete the total planning process—are outlined. The product of this planning phase is often referred to as the "plan for planning" and should identify each major task, persons responsible, resources committed, and time allotted for each. With clearly defined tasks, resources, responsibility, and time lines, it is then possible to (1) evaluate the planning endeavor as it occurs and (2) make desirable modifications to ensure achievement of the intended planning results.

If the "plan for planning" is to be developed and implemented, an organizational structure which assures effective planning is necessary, as well as input from all levels of the recreation department. In order to avoid ivory-towered and useless staff efforts, several things are needed. A planning staff should be given the tasks of developing major objectives, strategies, and planning premises, and submitting them to top administrators for review and approval. They should also be responsible for disseminating approved premises and strategies to people working throughout the recreation agency. Before major decisions are made, the recreation staff should be given the task of reviewing them and making recommendations. These few tasks can be advantageous in that they force

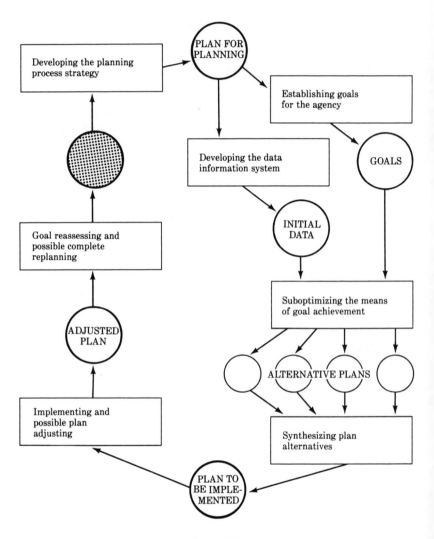

Figure 1. Comprehensive recreational planning model.

decision-makers to consider environmental factors present within the agency, and also prevent the staff from becoming a detached group.

A number of techniques—generally referred to as network analysis—can be effectively utilized in this phase of planning. Among the many variations of network analysis are the critical path method (CPM), the program evaluation review technique (PERT), flow or process charts, and milestone systems. While each

technique has certain advantages over others, PERT—probably
more than any other single technique—has had extensive application to recreation.

Development of the data information system   Development of
the data information system and establishment of goals for the
agency are shown in the model as interacting phases since many of
the initial data have direct implication for goals, and the establishment of goals affects the kinds of additional data that need to be
collected and analyzed. Four major purposes of the planning information system are

1. To store and retrieve data
2. To generate summaries
3. To generate alternatives
4. To evaluate and synthesize alternatives.

Four principles should guide development of the data system.
First, the data system must be comprehensive in scope and depth,
yet contain neither too many data nor the wrong data. Second, data
must be well-organized and easily accessible. Data are useless if
they cannot be quickly located and processed when needed. In many
cases, this simply means a carefully organized filing system; in a
large agency, a computer system is almost imperative. Third, the
data system must be continuously updated. Equally important to
adding new data is discarding unnecessary and outdated information. The fourth and final principle for development of the data system is twofold: (1) planning information must be shared, and (2) the
system must be well-coordinated with other data systems—for example, private or commercial recreation systems (Higgins and Conrad 1973:5–6).

In this phase it is most important to recognize that recreation
is a part of a complex system involving other highly interrelated
public, private, and commercial agencies reacting to other systems
(economic, transportation, health, etc.). Murphy (1975:67–68) points
out that the traditional organization of a municipality into separate
functions cannot cope with complex, interrelated social issues. This
traditional bureaucratic organization, characterized as a pyrami-
dal, centralized, functionally specialized mechanism, lacks relevance to the realities of contemporary technological society. The
rapidity and unexpectedness of social change make it extremely difficult for large bureaucracies, with their tight controls, outmoded
rules, and organizational rigidities to respond adequately to the new
demands of society.

Establishment of goals   Gold's (1973:133) planning text notes
that "a plan is meant to carry us toward a goal, but it is not a goal in

itself. A goal is not a plan, but something to be planned for. Goals are not achieved just because they are stated." The usefulness of the plan will depend on a general understanding and acceptance of the goals by all concerned. If this phase of the planning process does not include the views of the public, any plan is likely to fail. People not involved in the goal-formulation process at the beginning cannot be expected to understand or support its products.

Goals are conditioned by values that community members consider important. Social-research methods can be used to measure and analyze many of these values in order to test possible goals and objectives for community support. One alternative to conducting social research would be for the public recreation agency to develop goals and then subject them to public discussion. It should be noted, however, that this second approach is usually time-consuming and has inherent political risks.

Establishing the agency's goals may well be the most elusive, and the most challenging, step in the entire planning process; it is imperative, however, that well-defined goals be established before planning can proceed. If the goals are not ordered according to importance of resource priority, they must be accompanied by a brief statement of overarching principles that will permit decision-making when goal conflicts arise in either planning or implementation. Moreover, goals must be further defined into more specific objectives that can be measured. The more explicit objectives are, the more easily plans can be developed to attain them. Formulating objectives is a never-ending process of refinement and review to keep up with the changing nature of community values, technology, and local or national events.

Suboptimization of the means of goal achievement Suboptimizing the means of goal achievement is the heart of the planning process since the quality of the final product of the planning process will, in large part, be determined by the ability of planners to create viable alternatives from which the final plan can be synthesized. Each basic plan must have (1) a basic strategy by which goals can be achieved and (2) a service system for implementation.

A number of specific techniques have been used to generate alternatives, with brainstorming probably one of the most frequently used. The Advocate Team (Reinhard 1977:1-19)—a more recent technique involving a variety of persons—has proved very beneficial in overcoming time constraints. Probably the most exciting new techniques for generating alternatives are gaming and computer simulation. (Numerous sources on simulation can be found in the bibliography by Duke and Schmidt [1965:1-33].)

Information about past performance, the current situation, and the future is essential in helping to identify alternative courses of action and to evaluate them properly. Illustrative of types of past information collected are the following: success of programs, budget allocations, funding capabilities, and public relations. Information about the current situation, in addition, would include such matters as employee skills, competition, opportunities for cooperation with other local groups, interests of participants, and the local image of the public recreation department. Data about the future would include forecasts of selected economic trends, population demographics, and the availability of government funding.

Synthesizing plan alternatives   Synthesizing plan alternatives requires decision-makers to consider the various alternative components and blend them into the ultimate plan to be implemented. It is important that this phase be recognized as a synthetic process rather than as a process of choosing one alternative over another. Often the synthetic process creates additional alternatives that may be combinations of components from two or more initial alternatives.

The synthesis of plan alternatives is probably the most critical phase for total community involvement. Before the legally constituted decision-makers are called on to make decisions, they should have ample assessment data from the various echelons of the total community, including not only lay persons but also participants in various recreation programs and members of the professional recreation staff.

Implementations, with possible plan adjustment   Implementation must occur before the plan adjustment phase can be undertaken. As implementation gets underway, product-evaluation procedures must be initiated to provide data for decision-making in regard to plan adjustments. This phase is quite similar to the suboptimization phase since additional data—including product-evaluation data—will suggest plan-adjustment alternatives. This phase operates on the assumption that the agency's goals are still valid but that plan adjustments are needed to better meet them.

Lorange (1982:217-220) discusses several major environmental trends which can affect the implementation process. One trend that certainly would affect the recreation agency's plan would be the political situation. Political changes at the federal, state, and local level can all have an impact on recreation by influencing the availability of funding. Another issue of concern is related to changing values among local citizens, competitors, and political constituencies that might question the relevance of certain programs. A last trend would involve power shifts within the local community that might result in difficulty in implementing any plan that did not reflect the interests of those in power.

It should probably also be noted that some involvement of planners in the implementation process is desirable. In fact, this involvement may be a key to plan utilization and impact (Friedman and Hudson 1974:2–16; Johnson 1979:87–98). Planners must not be content with simply making plans, as Wildavsky (1973:127–53) has pointed out, but need rather to consider the extent of their success in terms of the things that happen as a result of planning implementation.

Goal reassessment, with possible complete replanning   The plan adjustment phase need not involve every phase of the comprehensive planning process. It is imperative, however, that goal reassessment be initiated periodically to surface indications for recycling the complete planning process. A common problem among organizations is that of remaining relevant; hence, periodic reassessment is essential.

Evaluation and planning   Evaluation has not been included as a separate phase in the comprehensive recreational planning model because it must permeate much of the planning process. First, there must be continuous evaluation throughout the planning process to allow for modification and improvement as planning progresses. Second, the comprehensive recreational plan—product of the planning process—must be evaluated as it is completed. Finally, an evaluation system is an essential element of any comprehensive recreational plan to ensure improved outcomes that the plan is designed to produce throughout implementation.

People involvement and planning   The process of involving people extends to both lay persons and professionals and permeates much of the comprehensive recreational planning process. Many persons will be involved in providing baseline data that will be collected from individuals and organized groups and agencies in the community, because it seems logical to seek broad-based community involvement in delineating goals and setting priorities. However, the responsibility for developing alternatives for meeting these goals is a technical task demanding some expertise. It should rest primarily with the professional staff, though others might well be involved. Ultimately, representatives of the total community should share in the assessment of these alternatives by providing input data for final decision-making. Without participating in the planning process, professional recreation staff run the dual risk of (1) neither adequately identifying nor adequately satisfying needs and (2) having the comprehensive plan rejected by the public (Morrison 1970:175–78).

Application of the model   A recreation agency attempting to implement the model described would encounter a number of organizational blockages in addition to the general inertia that impedes any significant change. Two of these have been labeled "opportunistic decision-making" and "organizational maintenance" by Edward Banfield (1962:73-75).

Rather than lay out objectives, identify alternative courses of action, and formulate a plan, agencies extemporize, meeting each crisis as it arises. To plan requires lucid identification of goals or ends, but these may be difficult to achieve in a multifaceted public agency serving a diverse public. In the face of this difficulty, opportunistic decision-making becomes the standard mode of action (Banfield 1962:73-75). Although acceptable for decades, opportunistic decision-making must now be superseded by planning as resources become scarce and public demands for accountability increase.

Organizational maintenance—keeping the organization and its members going for the sake of keeping it going—is unfortunately usually perceived as more important than any substantive end or goal of the organization. Salmon perish in order to give birth to young; organizations, however, unlike salmon, prefer sterility to death (Banfield 1962:77). While never eliminated, this problem can be mitigated to some extent by involving the community in the planning process; though agency staff may be constrained by the phenomenon of organizational maintenance, a committee representative of the public will not be.

The third—and possibly most serious—difficulty with planning in a public recreation agency is a phenomenon observed in any governmental or quasi-governmental unit. Decisions are based on political considerations rather than on rational processes (Campbell 1968:365-57). This problem can probably never be entirely eliminated, but the absence of planning increases the occurrences of political choices, while increased planning should reduce such incidences. Without rational choices, decision-makers may be left with nothing other than political whims; however, faced with thoroughly delineated planning processes, they are more likely to make rational choices. Instead of political considerations being viewed as a limitation on planning in a recreation agency, planning could be regarded as a way of reducing political influence through the substitution of opportunities for rational, apolitical decisions.

Planning is not the sole conquering force for the array of challenges facing public recreation agencies; however, the model described does provide a potential structure through which an agency can systematically confront significant issues and prepare for the future.

References

Banfield, Edward C. 1962. Ends and means in planning. In *Concepts and issues in administrative behavior*, ed. Sidney Mailick and Edward H. Van Wess. Englewood Cliffs, N.J.: Prentice-Hall.

Campbell, Ronald F. 1968. Educational planning in the United States. In *Planning in Australian education*, ed. G.W. Bassett. Hawthorn, Victoria, Australia: Australian Council for Educational Research.

Chakraborty, Samir, and Gabriel David. 1981. Why managers avoid planning and what top management can do about it. In *The practice of planning*. New York: Van Nostrand Reinhold.

Conrad, Marion J., Kenneth Brooks, and George Fisher. 1973. A model of comprehensive educational planning. *Planning and Changing* 4 (Spring): 3–14.

Culbertson, Jack. 1967. State planning for education. In *Planning and effecting needed changes in education*, ed. Edgar L. Morphet and Charles O. Ryan. Denver: Designing Education for the Future: An Eight-State Study.

Duke, Richard D., and Allen H. Schmidt. 1965. *Operational gaming and simulation in urban research*. Lansing, Mich.: Continuing Education Service.

Ewing, David W. 1969. *The human side of planning*. New York: Macmillan.

Friedman, John, and Barclay Hudson. 1974. Knowledge and action: A guide to planning theory. *Journal of the American Institute of Planning* (January):2–16.

Gold, Seymour M. 1969. A goal-oriented approach to recreation planning. Paper read at Park and Recreation Ad-

ministrators Institute, 9-14 November, at University of California Extension, Davis.

Gold, Seymour M. 1973. *Urban recreation planning*. Philadelphia: Lea & Febiger.

Higgins, K. Ronald, and M. J. Conrad. 1973. *A data system for comprehensive planning in education*. Chicago: Project Simu-School.

Johnson, A.P. 1979. Requisites for planning utilization. *Planning and Changing* 10 (Summer):87–98.

Lockyer, K.G. 1967. *An introduction to critical path analysis*. New York: Pitman.

Lorange, Peter. 1982. *Implementation of strategic planning*. Englewood Cliffs, N.J.: Prentice-Hall.

Morrison, Larry B. 1970. Neighborhood initiated plans: What planning with people means in the inner city. In *Planning 1970*. Chicago: American Society of Planning Officials.

Murphy, James F. 1975. *Recreation and leisure service*. Dubuque, Ia.: William C. Brown.

Reinhard, Diane. 1977. Methodology development in input evaluation using advocate and design teams. Ph.D. diss., Ohio State University.

Reinharth, Leon, Jack Shapiro, and Ernest Kallman. 1981. *The practice of planning*. New York: Van Nostrand Reinhold.

Steiner, George, 1979. *Strategic planning*. New York: The Free Press.

Wildavsky, Aaron. 1973. If planning is everything, maybe it's nothing. *Policy Sciences* 4:127-53.

Zaltman, Gerald, and Robert Duncan. 1977. *Strategies for planned change*. New York: John Wiley and Sons.

Evaluating for Accountability

Christine Z. Howe

Decision making is an ever-present task in the lives of professionals in the park, recreation, and leisure field. However, it is difficult to remember a time when making those decisions was harder than today. Not only are we faced with more leisure alternatives from which to choose, but with ever-increasing leisure demands that must be met with (typically) decreasing or stabilized resources. Thus, it is critical that we make our decisions as rationally and justly as possible. A major tool to help us make better decisions is evaluation. We should not hesitate to attempt evaluation. We should not hesitate to attempt evaluation *ourselves*. We can no longer stand back and rely on persons external to our agencies or our field to evaluate for us.

Evaluation is a legitimate means of systematically collecting data to serve as the basis for informed planning, analysis, and policy making. At present, competing programs and services are speaking to the same "ears" that we are. We can and must use evaluation to improve our communication—and perhaps be listened to just a bit more closely than the others. Furthermore, we can use evaluation to communicate among ourselves. Michael Farley, of the Portland Bureau of Parks and Recreation, suggests that this type of group interaction is an integral part of park, recreation, and leisure services. This interaction is the very heart of *political activity*, defined here as the use of power and influence to affect the allocation of limited

This article is based on a paper presented at the annual meeting of the American Alliance for Health, Physical Education, Recreation and Dance, in Houston, Texas, 1982. The paper was also the basis for a chapter entitled "Program Evaluation: Phase Four of the Leisure Programming Cycle," in Christine Z. Howe and G. M. Carpenter, *Programming Leisure Services: A Cyclical Approach* (Englewood Cliffs, NJ: Prentice-Hall, 1985).

resources to achieve desired ends. Evaluation helps us to monitor what we have, struggle to get what we need, and persuade others that what is proposed is reasonable, efficient, effective, and worthy of investment.

Definition and purpose of evaluation

To help us be victors in this struggle, a number of questions must be examined. First, just what is evaluation? In its most basic sense, evaluation is the process of judging the merit, worth, or value of something. We participate in informal evaluation in our daily lives each time we select one course of action from among several alternatives. In the formal evaluation of leisure programs, we are much more scientific and rational: We strive to base our choices on objectively examined facts. We use systematic inquiry to determine the value of something. In a sense, we undertake a project in applied research. We are trying to solve a problem that is situation specific and often immediate. As professionals in the leisure field, it is our responsibility to use the evaluation process to help ourselves and to better serve our clientele.

What, then, is the *purpose* of evaluation? Why should we evaluate? Interest in evaluating park, recreation, and leisure programs has been evident in the literature of our field for two decades, an interest that is growing as we get deeper into this "era of accountability." We are competing with other human service agencies for shrinking resources. Because this competition is occurring while the demand for leisure services in particular is on the rise, leisure service professionals are being compelled to be as efficient and effective as possible; the evaluation process can enable us to revise and improve our programs for the purposes of decision making and accountability. When we are accountable, we are *responsible*, and evaluation helps us to demonstrate responsible behavior. When we are efficient, we are able to show that we have used our resources prudently. When we are effective, we have facilitated a leisure experience that is satisfying, fulfilling, and meaningful to the participant.

By being responsible in this manner, we can evaluate in order to improve and justify our programs. We can meet the demands made by external authorities while documenting just exactly what it is that we do. Then our decisions should indeed be rational and factually based.

Evaluation in the programming cycle

Within leisure service delivery systems, the elements that can be evaluated include facilities, policies, sites, and personnel. But where does evaluation fit into the leisure programming cycle? The first phase of the leisure programming cycle is the assessment of client needs and interests. Preliminary information collection may take several forms. Some agencies conduct formal participant surveys through interviews or questionnaires. Other organizations merely seek information informally from participants at the end of a program. Others rely on the observations, intuition, or experience of the professional staff, and still others use citizen advisory boards to get opinions about programs. Whatever means or combination of means is used, the important thing is to determine the needs and interests of the clientele. The key is to systematically record information about leisure awareness, attitudes, needs, patterns, and interests and to use—not shelve—the results. Such data will help to broaden the base of support for leisure programs that is so very much needed today.

The second phase of the programming cycle is the planning or development of the program. If leisure opportunities are unavailable elsewhere, a responsive agency will plan new or additional programs to meet the expressed desires of its clientele. In practical terms, this usually means re-allocating existing resources or limiting new programs to those that are likely to be economically self-sufficient. Sound evaluation techniques can assist in certain operational aspects of this planning phase: gathering and storing demographic and attitudinal information; reviewing past evaluations and reports; obtaining participation ratings; budgeting personnel time; and accounting for program income and expenditures. Such information allows for decision making to be based on facts, not guesswork.

The third phase of the programming cycle is implementation—actually providing leisure experiences to clients. The fourth phase is evaluation. An evaluation that occurs during the implementation or the actual conduct of the program is called a *formative* evaluation and is undertaken for the improvement and revision of the program. An evaluation that occurs after the completion of the leisure program is summative, a final judgment of the merit or worth of a program. The type of evaluation used depends on the evaluative purpose. Given current concerns about accountability, it is wise to evaluate both formatively and summatively to provide the depth of data that is increasingly being demanded to justify programs and expenditures.

The fifth phase of the cycle is to modify the program based on information acquired in the first four phases. Figure 1 illustrates the ongoing, continuous nature of the programming cycle.

Internal evaluation in parks and recreation

Until recently, evaluations of leisure programs were generally undertaken by persons external to the agency. Although the relative merits of internal versus external evaluation continue to be debated

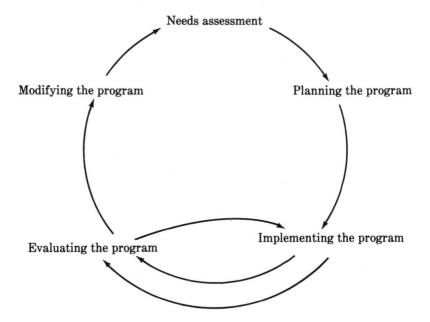

Figure 1. The leisure programming cycle.

in the literature, internal evaluation is preferable for several reasons.

First, evaluation should do more than meet external mandates for accountability; it is an internal service responsibility. The approaches that have been created to meet this responsibility suit the needs of the internal evaluator and were designed to be applied by the internal evaluator. If an evaluator has been trained to evaluate dispassionately, there is no reason for his or her credibility to come under question. Those who are closest to the leisure experience are best able to evaluate the effectiveness of a recreation program.

Second, the internal evaluator will be most sensitive to the intrinsic aspects of the leisure experience. He or she is likely to have developed, implemented, and facilitated the program and will bring a professional's insight to its evaluation. Participants' intrinsic motivators include the following:

1. Perceived freedom in selecting activities
2. Feelings of personal competence
3. Preference for activities that are commensurate with abilities
4. Relaxation
5. Novelty
6. Escape from stress or routine

7. Optimum arousal
8. Interplay of achievement and avoidance
9. Social interaction.

These complex psychological variables require subtle measurement, and such subtlety is likely to be in the repertoire of the internal evaluator.

Third, the internal evaluator can rely on professional standards and first-hand knowledge of the agency to develop a systematic, unbiased evaluation. Although the evaluation process still leaves the recreation programmer with choices to make, it provides a basis for rational decisions founded on facts.

Evaluation and policy

As useful as evaluation findings are to the programmer, they can be even more useful when communicated to all levels of the agency. The choices made by a programmer as an internal evaluator are generally limited to specific program goals and objectives, such as participant satisfaction, program leadership, costs, and strengths and weaknesses. However, when evaluative information is collected and shared with those at the policy level, it helps to establish accountability. Information from the programmer can be used by the administrator to describe the capabilities of the leisure service delivery system and to explain and justify activities, programs, and services.

The shift to utilization-focused evaluation

In the leisure services field, early approaches to evaluation were based on a particular definition of evaluation and on the need to isolate the effects of programs on behavior; they did not take account of real-world constraints on the evaluation setting or of the practical needs of the evaluation audience—those who were expected to use the data to make decisions. As a result, evaluation findings often went unused. As formal evaluation began to be performed internally and viewed in relation to practical decision making as well as methodological accuracy, the *utility* of evaluation findings increased in importance.

The growing role of evaluation in program planning and development has led to a change in emphasis from design-focused to utilization-focused evaluation. Design-focused evaluation is based on predetermined goals and objectives, relies on an experimental or quasi-experimental research design, and applies a single method of data collection. It is useful in determining what a program *should* be, or the degree to which a program is what it was officially intended to be. Utilization-focused evaluation, in contrast, is grounded in the real-world constraints of a program's operation and structure. Utilization-focused evaluation takes account of the actual program environment, and it responds to the information needs of the evaluation audience.

Interactionist perspective

Because it responds to the dynamic and spontaneous aspects of leisure, utilization-focused evaluation lends itself to an interactionist perspective, which uses multiple methods of data collection and nonexperimental evaluation designs. An interactionist approach allows the evaluator to view the program from the perspective of a number of people; to rely on a range of information sources; and to take account of non-controlled or unanticipated events, which we know occur quite often in leisure programs. The result is a broad-based description of what is happening in a program, rather than an analysis of the degree to which objectives were met. The descriptive information becomes the basis for program "goals" that reflect how the program actually operates. This approach incorporates the flexibility that the leisure programmer needs; for example, a program can be changed in midstream without any penalty for unexpected events.

Although interactionism works particularly well with the utilization-focused evaluation approach, it can also be used with the design-focused approach when non-controlled designs incorporating multiple methods of data collection in the real-world environment are employed.

Implications for the practicing recreator

Evaluation is a dynamic and systematic process for describing and judging the value of a program for the purpose of making factually based decisions. The evaluation process occurs in the real world and uses social science research techniques to collect, analyze, and interpret information. In leisure services, evaluation has come to be a part of the program planning and development cycle and an essential aspect of program management. From an external perspective, evaluation enables an agency to be accountable to its funding sources and its clients. From an internal perspective, evaluation allows the agency to revise and improve its programs.

What are the implications for the practicing recreator? During this era of limited resources, a number of educators and practitioners are developing, using, and disseminating evaluation models and procedures to facilitate factually based decision making. What is essential is that recreators take a proactive role and use the tools of evaluation now. Unless recreation professionals heed the call for accountability and program improvement, the chances for our continued survival may be seriously diminished.

Application section:
Highlights of evaluation techniques

The concluding section of this article is designed to help you study a problem in leisure programming at your own agency. Figure 2 summarizes the steps. *Begin by writing down on a separate sheet the evaluation questions that you want to ask.*

Most leisure agencies have a written philosophy or mission statement that guides the overall direction of the organization. Typically, the staff then writes goals or general statements of purpose that are in keeping with the mission. These goals are further refined into operational objectives or action statements for which the organization can be held accountable. The philosophy, goals, and objectives of the organization can be used to determine which evaluation questions to ask, inasmuch as these written statements reflect what the agency is supposed to be doing. In other words, what an evaluator would want to know should be grounded in the agency's mission, goals, and objectives, assuming that the leisure programs reflect the agency's mission, goals, and objectives.

Once the evaluation questions have been decided upon, the next step is to determine what evidence should be collected to obtain the answers. Such evidence may be descriptive or judgmental. Descriptive evidence may, for example, portray the participants in the program; describe interactions that occur in a recreational class; illustrate the context or environment of the leisure experience; or report the impact of an activity on the clientele. Judgmental evidence includes (1) statements of how well predetermined standards have been met and (2) professional judgments rendered by consultants or experts about the merit of the leisure program. *As the second step in the evaluation process, write down what kinds of evidence you will search for to answer the evaluation questions you have chosen.*

---

1. Choose the focus of your evaluation—the questions that you wish to ask.

2. Determine the kinds of evidence that are necessary to answer these questions.

3. Assess the resources that will be necessary—and available—to conduct the evaluation.

4. List potential audiences and rank them according to priority.

5. Decide on techniques for gathering data.

6. Choose techniques for analyzing data.

7. Determine the most appropriate means for reporting the findings.

Figure 2. Steps in a model evaluation process.

Before you get too far into the evaluation process, it is important realistically to consider the available resources. Some of the resources that an evaluation requires include the personnel time for those involved in the process; money for salaries of the evaluator, secretarial support, and consultants; and money for supplies, postage, duplication, and telephone calls. A major non-monetary cost is the interpersonal "expense": evaluation may have negative connotations and is sometimes perceived as threatening. Staff members may feel that their privacy is being invaded or that evaluation is just another burden for already overworked individuals. *As the next step in the process, write down the resources that you are likely to need—and have available—for your evaluation.*

Another factor to be considered is the evaluation audience. For whom is the evaluation being conducted? Who has an interest in the leisure program? Who needs to know the results of the evaluation? Is the funding or governing board the primary evaluation audience? Or is it the participants, their parents, or the programmer? If there are limited resources for the evaluation, how would the potential audiences be ranked in terms of priority? *As the next step, list—and rank—potential audiences.*

Thus far, we have identified accountability as the purpose of our evaluation. We have also determined the evaluation questions we are going to ask and what evidence we are going to search for. In addition, we have indicated what resources we require to conduct the evaluation and listed the potential audiences. Therefore, our next step is to choose techniques for collecting information.

The choice of data collection methods should be governed by the nature of the evidence that is desired. Methods commonly used by evaluators include written questionnaires consisting of both open- and closed-ended questions; face-to-face interviews; telephone interviews; participant observation; and the use of written documents or other artifacts. Books on programming, research methods, and management in leisure services provide thorough discussions of the strengths and weaknesses of each of these means of data collection. Suffice it to say that we want to employ the most valid and reliable data collection methods that are available. *As your next step, list your data gathering techniques.* Keep in mind that the strategies you select should be appropriate to the kinds of facts you are seeking.

Once the information is gathered, it must be analyzed. The nature of the data is the primary consideration in selecting the data analysis technique. For example, if numerical data are gathered, then quantitative analysis—ranging from simple frequency counts and percentages to averages to correlations—may be done. However, in addition to the nature of the information, the information needs of the audience must be taken into account: Complex statistical analyses are useless to individuals who do not have the background to interpret them.

Journalistic or qualitative information calls for techniques such as content analysis or critical review. The key is to synthesize the volume of information so that it is comprehensible to the intended audience. This may mean, for example, making descriptive comparisons of program change over time or correlating program impact with participant satisfaction. *As the next step in your evaluation, list some data analysis techniques that would be appropriate for the type of information that you want to gather.* Also make note of your perceptions of your primary evaluation audience.

Finally, evaluation results must be made available to the audience. Thus, it is necessary to select a means of reporting the evaluation findings. Again, the nature of the results determines how they will be most effectively disseminated; in addition, the reporting techniques must be appropriate to the recipients of the evaluation information.

The evaluation results may be a progress report or a final summation and may be expressed in a variety of ways: written or oral, technical or nontechnical, descriptively or prescriptively. Visual and audio aids may be used to communicate the results: charts or graphs, overhead transparencies, slides, tapes, photographs, and recorded interviews or testimony. Well-chosen dissemination techniques will encourage the translation of the results into decisive action. *As your final step, list some evaluation reporting techniques that you feel would best express your results.*

What we have completed is a generic or basic evaluation process. The model we have followed underlies all of the more specialized evaluation models or approaches used in our field.

Program Evaluation as a Political Tool

Michael Farley

Program evaluation is the process of determining program performance for the purpose of improving service delivery. There are
many reasons why evaluation is an important and necessary tool for
administrators. As a measurement tool, program evaluation helps
determine how well objectives are being met. It provides a framework for determining program successes and failures. It can be used
to redefine the means for achieving goals. It can also create a standard means to collect information from different data bases that
can later be used to undertake further research on program performance. In a broad sense, program evaluation is an aid to rational
and informed decision-making.

 The evaluation process also assists the administrator in another way. As a communication technique, program evaluation
helps the administrator meet the political challenges that exist for
any agency. Evaluation provides a means for linking the public,
staff, agency, or educational administrators, and elected officials in
the tasks of planning and delivering services and accounting for the
use of public funds. As a communication device, program evaluation
can become a persuasive political tool.

The political environment

A closer look at the political nature of the service agency environment provides several clues for recognizing how program evaluation
can influence the political process. As purveyors of programs, administrators move in a political world. They make decisions with

This article is reprinted with permission from the *Journal of Physical Education,
Recreation & Dance* (April 1984): 64–67. The *Journal* is a publication of the American
Alliance for Health, Physical Education, Recreation and Dance, 1900 Association
Drive, Reston, VA 22091.

other people to determine program purpose, content, and policy. The staff interacts with the public to learn about community needs. As public servants, they engage in decision-making processes with politicians to set program priorities and compete for limited public funds. These occasions relate to the political process because each interaction touches the heart of political activity; i.e., the use of power and influence to affect the allocation of limited resources to achieve desired outcomes. Deciding how to use what we have, struggling to get what is needed, and persuading others that what is proposed is reasonable, efficient, publicly supported, and worthy of investment all require political skills.

Program evaluation can arm professionals well for these political jousts. As a political tool, evaluation is not presented here as a means to manipulate information to gain support for preconceived notions about tax-supported services. Rather, it is a legitimate aid to the administrator to develop support for well-informed program decisions. In this sense, evaluation functions as a communication process which, to be an effective political tool, must run throughout the course of a program's yearly life-cycle.

Setting the stage for the political drama

For program evaluation to serve as a political tool, certain characteristics must be present in the evaluation effort. First, evaluation must be an on-going *process*, not a one-time exercise. Second, evaluation should not be conducted to prove or disprove an activity, but to improve the conduct of the activity. This orientation is essential if program staff are to be engaged in an open communication process. Third, evaluation should be designed to measure actual program outcomes against prestated program goals. Such a process gives evaluation participants a common orientation in determining the relative value of program results. This goal-oriented approach is composed of several activities: setting goals and measurable objectives, implementing programs, collecting information, measuring performance, and adjusting programs according to findings.

A fourth characteristic is broad-based participation. Program evaluation should provide opportunities for players at all levels within the agency to evaluate. A participative environment is an essential part of the evaluation process, building trust within the organization and developing commitment to the effort.

Two additional necessary characteristics are utility and simplicity. Grandiose evaluation methodologies which delight the academician may foil the practitioner. If evaluation is to be true to its mission of improving services, then the methodologies it employs and the information it produces must be useful to those who need specific program data. Information must be relevant, readily usable, and in a form which relates to daily operations.

It cannot be stated strongly enough that the intended purpose of the evaluation effort will greatly influence the information that needs to be generated. If an administrator is looking toward budget justification, then a high premium will be placed on cost/benefit analysis. If staff wish to determine how effectively a program is meeting user expectations, then survey instruments are most useful. Of the many reasons for evaluating programs, justifying budgets and meeting community needs are only two.

Depending on the purpose for which evaluation is intended, different evaluation models and techniques have different strengths. Further, different purposes for evaluation are not mutually exclusive and are oftentimes complementary. A city council member, during a budget hearing, may be interested in the cost/benefit analysis of a particular program, but may become truly enlightened when a user group follows the analysis with an expression of support for the program that they helped evaluate. Information of one kind can support and explain data of another type. The professional can blend qualitative and quantitative information to more completely portray the performance of a program to the intended audience.

Measuring what has been achieved and generating information that is relevant to the intent of the evaluation provide no guarantee that the findings will be used by program practitioners. Notwithstanding problems of accepting evaluation findings as credible and legitimate, evaluation results must be interpreted clearly so the program manager knows what to do with what is produced. The evaluation process should provide for a briefing exercise that allows the findings to be discussed and program adjustment options to be explored. The daily flurry of activity that characterizes any sports office or community center will pale the interest of the practitioner in reading a 40-page report, no matter how interestingly prepared. It is one thing to *generate* relevant information; it is quite another to know how to *use* it.

These characteristics are important values for the program evaluation effort to promote. Not only do they impact on whether or not the evaluation effort will be successful, they also set the stage for program evaluation to influence the political process of distributing limited resources to achieve intended outcomes.

As the stage is set, evaluation nurtures the development of four objectives which are essential to the life of successful programs; *accountability, legitimacy, public support,* and *effective communication of results.* These are the brass rings for which program directors must stretch.

Accountability

Program leaders are accountable for specific results when concrete goals and objectives are identified and program performance is measured. As planning tools, goals and objectives set a framework for the services that are to be provided. As management tools, performance measures assist managers in evaluating the delivery of services. Without realistic goals and measurable objectives, it is difficult to know and communicate to others whether we are functioning efficiently and effectively or even if the agency is providing the services the public demands.

Program leaders should also be accountable to their supervisors as well as to the public and political leadership for how public monies are spent and to what effect. By comparing program performance to planned objectives, the director can document the extent to which programs are successful, and adjust the program accordingly. Managers responsible for revenue producing facilities, for example, often project program revenues for each fiscal quarter. By determining how the facility performed over a three month period, the manager may wish to refocus resources on marketing activities or change program rates to more adequately capture revenues during peak programming hours.

Finally, practitioners determine how program accountability is to be achieved by designing a reporting process as part of the program evaluation exercise. Evaluative efforts require interaction with the public, staff and administrators in setting objectives, gathering information, reviewing the outcomes and communicating the results. Program evaluation therefore functions as a political tool by establishing accountability (a) for program performance, (b) to a variety of participants, and (c) through certain communication processes.

Legitimacy

If program accountability is achieved, the practitioner is halfway home in establishing the legitimacy of evaluation findings and recommendations for adjustments. Legitimacy in this sense refers to the degree of acceptability and credibility conferred by staff, administrators, politicians and the public on the information generated through the evaluation process.

Programs become misguided when objectives are vague and the means to achieve them are conflicting among program staff and supervisory personnel. When the process of evaluation produces a clear definition of objectives and the indicators to measure them, practitioners short-circuit many service delivery problems. They have invested themselves in designing the program. They have a personal stake in seeing that the program succeeds. When agreement is reached in this initial phase of the evaluation process, practitioners are more likely to accept the findings of program performance measurement. Similarly, establishing a common set of expectations greatly contributes to a more productive treatment of program adjustments.

An evaluation exercise for summer swim programming in Portland, Oregon, engaged pool staff in conducting user surveys. Staff participated with the evaluator in designing questionnaires and soliciting responses from participants. Following the tabulation and analysis of the results, the director and staff agreed to change swim schedules for certain user groups. Previous to the evaluation exercise, similar program adjustments had been suggested by staff, but were not implemented.

Evaluation findings can legitimize recommendations for program adjustments when the evaluation process engages those who are directly involved with the program. Unacceptable suggestions for changing program policy can become credible when the process for considering program questions invests the practitioners in a common discovery task.

Legitimacy also plays an important role in garnering the political support of others more highly placed in the decision-making process and further removed from a particular program. Practitioners who have a data base regarding resources, program needs, and community interests are in a good position to shape judgments and priorities of other decision-makers regarding their programs. Evaluation can develop the legitimacy of recommendations by providing information that cries out for program change. It can demonstrate that a pet program of an administrator has little public support. It can also show where programs need to be altered or buttressed by additional resources. Further, evaluation can show how and why the provision of certain services is better left to organizations other than the tax-supported agency or institution.

As a communication process, program evaluation can build legitimacy for recommendations among practitioners who may not have been open to certain program adjustments. As an information tool, evaluation can help reach those influential persons detached from the program who need hard evidence before proposed program adjustments are perceived as legitimate.

Public support

Public support for programs is a key to determining successful outcomes to political decision-making. Like accountability and legitimacy, public support for programs can be a product of the program evaluation process. Opportunities for cultivating program support and fine-tuning services occur at three critical points in the life-cycle of a program. Two of these points fall within the evaluation process itself.

The first opportunity occurs during information-gathering activities. It is the process of collecting information which sets the stage for building public interest in the evaluation exercise among participants and survey respondents. People like to be asked their opinion. They like to know that their opinions matter. Further, it is important for confidence-building in the institution that it demonstrate it is well-organized in gathering information, and that it cares about the people it serves.

A second opportunity for developing support occurs when program outcomes are reviewed by advisory groups. Here practitioners can engage public groups in a problem-solving exercise that focuses on program adjustment.

The third opportunity point for cultivating program support is presented during the budget process. If evaluation efforts have successfully measured program performance and engaged public groups along the way, administrators are in a better position to advocate program continuation, expansion, or major policy adjustments. Constituent groups knowledgeable of efforts to improve programs can play a prominent and persuasive role in the public forum. The process of evaluation creates opportunities for practitioners to inform user groups about issues in a methodical way. When the budget discussions begin, a new perspective can be interjected into the conversation by citizens who have invested in the evaluation.

Communicating the results

A discussion of program evaluation as a political tool would not be complete without recognizing the substantial challenge posed to administrators in effectively communicating the results of evaluation efforts. The very qualitative nature of many public services provides an additional burden on practitioners for effective communication. The call for quantifiable data and the increased value placed on cost-effectiveness require administrators to articulate the value of programs that serve the public—whether child, youth, or adult.

The key ingredient to effective communication is knowing the information needs of individuals in the political process. Particularly in budgetary proceedings, cost/benefit data holds a prominent place in justifying programs. However, not all decisions in the political process are budgetary. Other information needs that impact on the decision making process include the opinions of program staff, user groups, and elected officials. Statistical data represents a third kind of information necessary for determining demographic characteristics of service areas and relative need levels for certain services. According to the purpose for which evaluation is intended, the extent to which program advocates provide the kind of information needed by a particular audience will influence their effectiveness as communicators in the political process.

Evaluation involves discovery. It is in this exercise of "finding" that program evaluation empowers its participants. Faced with an increased demand to do more for less, the practitioners find that the evaluation process becomes increasingly significant as a source of knowledge and direction. It provides the administrator with an important tool to refine programs, create new ones, and drop the losers. As a political tool, the evaluation process can build account-ability for program performance. It can legitimize program adjustments. It can also assist the administrator in cultivating a well-informed constituency which contributes to the continued improvement of programs and advocates. Finally, it can provide the information necessary for effective communication in the political environment for the provision of public services. The real political power of evaluation is process: developing information and engaging participants in the evaluative exercise.

PART 2

Personnel and Productivity

Legal and Social Aspects of Personnel Selection

William R. McKinney

The capability of a public park and recreation agency to offer programs and provide facilities that are consistent with the needs of its constituents depends on personnel selection procedures that can identify job candidates who are (1) skillful in planning and delivering recreation services and (2) representative of the various publics the agency serves. The United States seems to be entering an era of new standards for the provision of public recreation opportunities. Research undertaken during the past two decades indicates that non-work time has increased (Talpert 1981); a wider range of individual leisure patterns has developed (Kelly 1981); and attendance at public parks and outdoor recreation areas has continued to rise (NRPA 1982). Coupled with heightened demand for park and recreation services is the requirement that those services reflect the diversity of recreation consumers. The human rights movements of the past twenty years have led to a greater appreciation of people, of pluralism, and of the right to self-determination (Goodale 1982). As members of the same community become less likely to share a common background (Gold 1973), public park and recreation agencies will have to be increasingly flexible in their services. The complexity of these and other issues affecting recreation has led some experts in the field to suggest that of all the tasks confronting public recreation agencies, none is more pressing than the selection of competent personnel (Culkin and Kirsch 1986; Rodney and Toalson 1981).

Private vs. public personnel management
The environments in which organizations must function vary, as do the parameters within which they must conduct their personnel selection programs. In contrast to a private sector organization, the

park and recreation agency is characterized by its accessibility to its constituents. Politicians, racial and ethnic groups, special-interest groups, and the media constantly scrutinize the personnel practices of public park and recreation managers. The proximity of this public agency to the service population significantly shapes its personnel practices and decisions (Couturier 1986; Levine and Nigro 1975). Stated simply, the political, social, and economic conditions of the immediate geographic region may determine, to a great extent, who is hired in a public recreation agency.

Proliferation of trained professionals

The problems of increasing demand for expanded and diverse recreation services and environmental pressures on the selection system are compounded by the proliferation of trained professionals in the park and recreation field. More than 50,000 college students are currently enrolled in programs specializing in parks and recreation (Henkel 1985). Competition for positions in park and recreation agencies is acute and will only increase as colleges and universities continue to graduate trained leaders. This trend intensifies the need for greater effectiveness in the personnel selection programs of public park and recreation agencies.

Objectives of this discussion

All park and recreation agencies are concerned about the people they employ as well as about those they serve, and the agencies have a moral and legal obligation to use fair employee selection practices. To act otherwise is to risk investigation or litigation by federal and state organizations. In addition, unfair selection practices foster resentment and frustration among employees and damage the agency's image among its constituents. However, what constitutes fair and equitable personnel selection is a source of increasing debate. This article is designed to

1. Describe the legal and social issues surrounding public personnel selection
2. Present a field experiment that demonstrates options in the selection decision
3. Discuss the empirical questions and legislative requirements that affect personnel selection in public park and recreation agencies.

Both fields—parks and recreation and personnel—have experienced dramatic growth in theory and practice during the past twenty years. This article describes contemporary psychological tools that will enable the park and recreation manager to translate theory into practice.

Legislative issues

The most sweeping legislation affecting personnel selection in this country is contained in Title VII, Section 703 of the Civil Rights Act of 1964. As amended by the Equal Employment Opportunity Act of 1972, Title VII applies to state and local governments; to all educational institutions, private employers, employment agencies, and unions with at least fifteen employees or members; and to joint labor-management apprenticeship and training programs. The statute stipulates that it is unlawful for an employer to refuse to hire, to discharge, or to discriminate in any employment practices because of an individual's race, color, religion, sex, or national origin (Civil Rights Act 1964).

In effect, this legislation pressured organizations (1) to identify what the courts interpreted as discrimination and (2) to open additional job opportunities for all groups. The Civil Rights Act also contained the following passage, which has directed employee selection research to date:

Notwithstanding any other provisions of this title, it should not be an unlawful practice for an employer ... to give and to act upon the results of any professionally developed ability test.

Despite the intent of the Civil Rights Act, its practical effect was to encourage the private sector to discontinue personnel testing programs altogether. Private employers were not willing to pay the bill for a validation program or to risk a potential lawsuit for using selection tests (Davey 1986). In public park and recreation agencies, the effect of this legislation is quite the opposite. Public employers are *required* by Equal Employment Opportunity Commission (EEOC) regulations and by existing employment laws to use job-related, standardized, and scorable selection methods. The most significant selection regulations are presented in the "Uniform Guidelines on Employee Selection Procedures" (EEOC 1978), which govern all employment decisions. The "Uniform Guidelines" state that (1) any criteria used to screen or select applicants or to promote employees must be reasonably related to the entry-level requirements of the position for which the applicant is applying; and (2) there should be empirical evidence that demonstrates the validity of the selection criteria. Therefore, personnel selection examinations for public agencies represent not only the most feasible way to deal with a large and diverse group of applicants, but also the only way to conform fully with the law (Dunnette and Borman 1979; Hill 1980; Ledvinka and Schoenfeldt 1978).

Social issues

The use of personnel selection examinations in the public park and recreation agency is not, however, as automatic as simply establishing the validity of the process. EEOC legislation has designated five groups of people as protected under Title VII: blacks, Hispanics, American Indians, Asian Pacific Islanders, and women (Schaeffer 1978). Conflict is increasing between those who believe that the civil rights legislation was intended to ensure equal *results* for protected groups *now* (Idelson 1979) and those who believe that the legislation calls for equal *opportunities* for all individuals *forever* (Learner 1980). Those who are committed to "equal results now" regard tests in general, and valid tests in particular, as unjustified and mean-spirited. They view selection tests as a covert, but legal, approach to preventing the full integration of minority groups into the employment ranks of an organization. The anger of people demanding the abandonment of selection examinations is not completely unfounded. Davey (1984) reports:

It was once popularly thought that the problem with written ability tests was that they were "culturally biased" and that this could be cured simply by debiasing them. . . . Two decades of attempts to eliminate the elusive quality of "cultural bias" have had little results. . . . Only when educational, employment and social conditions have been equalized and the vestiges of past discrimination have been wiped out will tests and other valid evaluation procedures be finally and genuinely free of adverse impact.

Validity and representation

These two issues, the inclusion of protected groups in selection results and the validity of the selection criteria, are the paramount concerns in public park and recreation selection decisions. The field experiment described in the next section was undertaken to explore the role of a written selection examination in determining the composition of the park and recreation work force, while avoiding adverse impact, and to evaluate the benefits of the examination for park and recreation agencies. While effective procedures for the development of generally valid park and recreation selection examinations are described elsewhere (see McKinney 1983), special measures are necessary to ensure that selected candidates are also representative of the racial, ethnic, cultural, and gender characteristics of the constituents that they will serve. Traditional selection programs have emphasized accurate measurement and predictive efficacy as final goals; in this field experiment, these conditions merely set the stage for the decision-making process in personnel selection.

Field experiment

A personnel selection examination was developed for a maintenance position within a public park and recreation agency in one of the nation's twelve largest cities. To develop the examination, six incumbents of the maintenance position were asked to divide the job universe into seven general content domains (knowledge areas). The areas identified were

1. Principles
2. Tools
3. Safety
4. Blueprints
5. Materials
6. Math
7. Dealing with others.

Next, the panel of six systematically developed a selection examination composed of ninety-two items to cover the job content. The test development process involved pretesting, item analysis, and reliability measures. The selection examination was then administered to 152 applicants for the maintenance position.

At the time of initially applying for the position and before taking the test, the applicants were asked to complete a voluntary equal employment opportunity information questionnaire. The questionnaire asked the applicant to specify personal characteristics that were protected by the Civil Rights Act of 1964: age, sex, race, ethnic group, citizenship, and any sensory, mental, or physical disabilities.

Results   The final selection examination included ninety-two test items. Of the 152 job applicants, the lowest score was nineteen items correct and the highest score was eighty-four correct. The overall test difficulty was 58.55, which was approximately the midpoint of the examination. When difficulty falls at the midpoint, the range of scores is usually greatest, and the likelihood is greater that the test is discriminating between more knowledgeable and less knowledgeable candidates. The reliability measure of the test indicated that the examination was satisfactory for use in the selection of applicants.

To assess whether the examination was sensitive to differences among applicants based on age, race, ethnic group, or disability (all applicants were male and United States citizens), total and content domain scores were compared. Age and disability did not create significant differences between groups; however, when applicants were compared by race and ethnic origin, the scores differed substantially. Black and Hispanic applicants' scores were significantly lower than those of other applicants on three of the content domains (principles, tools, materials), which contained the majority of test items, as well as on the overall test.

Identifying the alternatives   The American Psychological Association (1980) suggests that scores achieved on a selection examination developed according to the procedures described in the field experiment have a linear relationship to job success. In other words, a park and recreation agency that bases its selection on top-down raw scores will, with a good deal of consistency, choose those applicants that have more job knowledge than others. However, if the instrument used in the selection procedure is sensitive to differences among applicants based on protected characteristics, as in this instance, then the agency has three choices:

1. Disregard (not use) the examination scores as a selection criterion
2. Choose applicants on the basis of the examination raw scores, but be prepared to defend the validity of the examinations in court
3. Group applicants based on minority and majority status and select from the top score down within each separate list.

Disregarding the examination   Disregarding the examination results is rarely a viable alternative for a park and recreation agency. Since the passage of the Civil Rights Act, all employment practices that result in the selection of an applicant for a job are legally regarded as "tests." Personal history and background requirements, specific educational or work history requirements, scored interviews, and scored application forms, when used as bases for selecting among applicants, must demonstrate validity. Since validity is difficult to establish in personnel selection, disregarding the examination may leave the park and recreation agency without any selection criteria that meet the requirements of the current legislative mandates. The field experiment suggests that the procedure created a reliable examination that measures relevant, entry-level job knowledge; thus, one of the two remaining alternatives appears to be the logical selection procedure.

Top-score-down   Choosing applicants from the top raw score down is a legitimate solution if expected job performance is the sole basis for selection and if the agency seeks only to employ the most knowledgeable applicants. However, according to the "Uniform Guidelines on Employee Selection Procedures,"

a selection rate for any racial, ethnic, or sex subgroup which is less than four-fifths of the rate for the group with the highest rate will generally be regarded as evidence of adverse impact (EEOC 1978).

For example, if an employer used a selection procedure that resulted in 60% of the black applicants and 80% of the white applicants being hired, the ratio 60/80 would not be equal to or greater than 4/5; thus, adverse impact and a prima facie violation of the Civil Rights Act would be established (e.g., *Albemarle Paper Co. vs. Moody*). In this field experiment, choosing applicants from the top score down would not meet the four-fifths requirement of EEOC. Quite likely, then, the park and recreation agency could expect to be asked to defend its selection procedure in a court of law. Although the potential for litigation may cause an agency to reject the raw scores approach, the use of raw scores does provide the best alternative when an agency's principal goal is to employ only the most knowledgeable job applicants.

Separate list   Perhaps the most viable alternative for a public park and recreation agency is to group applicants based on race and ethnicity and to select applicants from the top score down for each subgroup. Schmidt (1981) and Davey (1984) have argued persuasively that hiring from the top score down by subgroup is a reasonable approach, and two recent Supreme Court decisions have confirmed the utility of this method. In *International Association of Firefighters v. City of Cleveland* (54 USLW 5005) and in *Sheet Metal Workers International Association v. Equal Employment Opportunity Commission* (54 USLW 4984), the Supreme Court ruled that past racial discrimination entitles minority workers to preference in hiring and promotion. The Court argued that racial and ethnic minorities deserved favored treatment even though the individuals concerned had not themselves been victims of discriminatory acts and even though they would "leapfrog" over equally qualified, non-Hispanic whites.

The study on which this article is based suggests that if park and recreation agencies group applicants into racial and ethnic subgroups and select applicants from the top score down from each list, full heterogeneity by race and ethnicity can be achieved. This procedure complies with the four-fifths rule of EEOC and is the best approach if the goal is to hire the most productive work force possible while achieving racial and ethnic balance.

A word on fairness   An employer can give meaning to test results either by construing a raw score as an indication that an applicant possesses specific knowledge, or by establishing separate lists that indicate each applicant's position in a clearly defined subgroup. How the test results are used depends on whether the agency must have someone who is, upon employment, fully capable of fulfilling the requirements of the position, or who is racially or ethnically representative of the agency's constituents—or both. Agencies with a history of egregious discrimination and existing selection practices that have had demonstrably adverse impacts should seriously consider the alternative of separate selection lists. Before using the separate list approach, however, an employer should first show that a protected group has been underutilized in the specific job.

Conclusion

As has been suggested, the present legal climate makes it imperative that public park and recreation organizations establish the validity of their selection decisions. Individual differences provide the basic rationale for selection. To be sure, the goal of the selection procedure is to capitalize on those differences to select applicants with the greatest number of characteristics judged important for job success. At some point in the personnel selection process, discussion will focus on two definitions of successful selection: technical expertise or social representation. Each agency must consider the legal and ethical ramifications of hiring from the top down using a full list of all job candidates or selecting from the top down using separate lists of majority and minority candidates. The ultimate choice rests with each agency, but in making the decision, the agency must consider the framework of the law, and the mandates of constituencies.

References

Albemarle Paper Co. v. Moody. U.S. Supreme Court Decision 422, U.S. 405, 10 FEP 1181.

American Psychological Association. 1980. *Principles for the Validation and Use of Personnel Selection Procedures,* 2nd ed. Washington, D.C.: American Psychological Association.

Couturier, J. 1986. "The Quiet Revolution in Public Personnel Laws." *Public Personnel Management* (May-June).

Culkin, D. F., and S. L. Kirsch. 1986. *Managing Human Resources in Recreation, Parks, and Leisure Services.* New York: Macmillan.

Davey, B. W. 1984. "Personnel Testing and the Search for Alternatives." *Public Personnel Management* (Winter).

———. 1986. "Personnel Testing and the Search for Alternatives." *Public Personnel Management* (May-June).

Dunnette, M. D., and W. G. Borman. 1979. "Personnel Selection and Classification Systems." *Annual Review of Psychology* 30.

Equal Employment Opportunity Commission. 1978. "Uniform Guidelines in Employee Selection Procedures." *Federal Register* 43.

Gold, S. 1973. *Urban Recreation Planning.* Philadelphia: Lea & Febiger.

Goodale, T. 1982. *A Decade of Difficult Tasks: Municipal Recreation in the Eighties.* Ontario, Canada: Ministry of Culture and Recreation.

Henkel, D. L. 1985. "Professionalization: The Saga Continues, 1955-1985." *Parks and Recreation* (August).

Hill, F. S. 1980. "Job Relatedness vs. Adverse Impact in Personnel Decision Making." *Personnel Journal* 33.

Idelson, E. M. 1979. *Eliminating Discrimination in Employment: A Compelling National Priority.* Washington, D.C.: Equal Employment Opportunity Commission.

Kelly, J. 1981. "Leisure and Family Change: 1960-1990." *Leisure Today* 52 (October).

Learner, B. 1980. "Employment Discrimination, Adverse Impact, Validity, and Equality." *Supreme Court Review,* vol. 31. Chicago: University of Chicago.

Ledvinka, J., and F. F. Schoenfeldt. 1978. "Legal Development in Employment Testing: Albemarle and Beyond." *Personnel Journal* 31.

Levine, C. H., and L. G. Nigro. 1975. "The Public Personnel System: Can Judicial Administration and Major Management Coexist?" *Public Administration Review* 35 (January and February).

Local 93, International Association of Firefighters v. City of Cleveland, ——— U.S. ———, 106 S. Ct. 3063 (1986).

Local 28, Sheet Metal Workers Interna-

tional Association et al. v. Equal Employment Opportunity Commission, ———— U.S. ————, 106 S. Ct. 3019 (1986).

McKinney, W. R. 1983. "The Content Validation of Personnel Selection Examination." *Journal of Parks and Recreation Administration* 4.

National Recreation and Park Administration. 1982. "Parks for the Year 2000: Increasing Urbanization and Decreasing Resources Will Demand More Innovative Park Design in the Years Ahead." *Network* 4 (Summer).

O'Leary, L. R. 1973. "Fair Employment, Sound Psychometric Practice and Reality: A Dilemma and a Partial Solution." *American Psychologist* 28.

Rodney, L. S., and R. F. Toalson. 1981.

Administration of Recreation, Parks, and Leisure Services. New York: John Wiley and Sons.

Schaeffer, R. G. 1980. *Nondiscrimination in Employment and Beyond.* No. 782. New York: Conference Board.

Schmidt, F. L. 1981. "Employment Testing: Old Theories and New Research Findings." *American Psychologist* 30.

Schmidt, F. L., A. C. Greenthal, J. S. Hunter, J. G. Berner, and W. F. Seaton. 1972. "Job Samples vs. Paper and Pencil Trade and Technical Tests: Adverse Impact and Employee Attitude." *Personnel Psychology* 30.

Talpert, R. 1981. "Looking Into the Future: Management in the 21st Century." *Management Review* 70 (March).

Personnel Evaluation: In Search of Valid Performance Standards

Ted Tedrick

It can easily be argued by both leisure service managers and academic theoreticians that the need for an effective management system has never been greater. Indicators of the future point the way to increasing stress on already fragile support networks. Public service managers, in particular, have had to adapt to shortages in materials and manpower during recent years as budgets in many cases have been pared to below subsistence levels. Doing the same with less has become commonplace, and evidence of the human toll taken by such conditions is readily available in the form of increased employee hypertension and the growth of stress-management seminars sponsored by industry.

As employees have frequently been required to assume new or varied tasks, the already muddled area of performance evaluation has become more complex, while at the same time assuming a higher degree of importance within the organization context. The variables affecting performance shift as job responsibilities change; a task once crucial to job success often becomes less significant as priorities are shuffled. Discretionary funds for meritorious performance are fewer, leading to even keener annual competition. Individual performance and goal attainment have become critical to the budget process, as higher level managers in private corporations and board members in the public sector have demanded a close scrutiny of all fiscal matters. In certain situations the decision of whom to retain, furlough, or terminate because of budget inconsistencies

From the *Journal of Park and Recreation Administration* 1, no. 3 (July 1983). Reprinted with permission from the Academy of Park and Recreation Administration.

may be directly based on recent performance appraisals, although reliance on seniority in such cases dominates. Students and critics of the evaluation process are in agreement that it is a costly and imperfect, yet essential, component of the personnel-management system that has undergone change as employee responsibilities have been altered for the reasons mentioned. Spooner and Johnson (1980:8) comment: "The real measure of management performance is how well it achieves objectives in a particular environment. Today the environment is more complex than in past decades. And it changes faster."

Appraisal systems examined

Performance appraisal has generally progressed from a focus on personality traits and other highly subjective elements to a more widely accepted usage of mutually-agreed-upon, quantifiable objectives that serve as the basis for measurement. Edginton and Williams (1978:382-84) have detailed the weaknesses of the personality trait rating scale as being poorly related to individual outputs and weighing all traits equally, when in reality particular aspects are more crucial to performance than others. Today, we appear to be less concerned about certain personality traits and more concerned about the ability of leisure-service managers to account for all funds expended, to develop successful marketing and public relations strategies, and to use manpower to increase efficiency.

Various MBO (management-by-objectives) systems have been discussed and suggested for implementation within governmental and commercial recreation organizations. The management-by-objectives approach attempts to measure in specific, quantifiable terms those goals established by the evaluatee in concert with his/ her supervisor. It seeks to improve upon traditional evaluation techniques by individualizing the process—a costly but in most cases more equitable method for all in the system.

Management by objectives is not without is critics. The very difficult task of qualifying results on all tasks undertaken presents frequent problems for those in a humanistic endeavor like leisure services (Rodney and Toalson 1981:71; Edginton and Williams 1978: 389-90). Rockwood (1982:186-88) has raised an additional point worth considering in relation to municipal agencies, namely the reluctance of many in the political arena to be "tied" to specific goals and timetables. Administrators may find themselves working for those who have a built-in distrust for a system that can hold one so nakedly accountable.

How then might performance evaluation be improved upon? Recognizing that any change within an organization is likely to meet with resistance, and acknowledging that time will be necessary to develop, administer, and modify any approach like MBO, the first step would be a desire to change current evaluation practices and a belief that evaluation can be responsible for improved employee performance and greater overall efficiency. Those conditions being present, we may then move to a careful analysis of mission statement and individual responsibility in search of valid standards for measuring performance.

Mission statement, impact areas, and competency measures

Alexander (1980:43-46) has proposed that three things are crucial if effective performance standards are to exist:

1. A mission statement must exist that is current and adequately reflects the purpose of the organization.
2. Each job within the organization must be studied so that critical impact areas or major areas of responsibility are known by employee and supervisor alike.
3. Measurable indicators of competent performance in each of the impact areas must be delineated and used in assessing worker strengths and weaknesses.

An accurate, up-to-date mission statement must exist in all organizations if meaningful evaluation is to follow. Because resources have become constricted, and professionals have decided to reduce program duplication, many leisure-service agencies are making the conscious decision that they can no longer be all things to all people, and steps are being taken that reflect this shift in priorities. Parks divisions strapped by labor cutbacks have had to reexamine past standards. Annual painting and other forms of preventive maintenance, for example, have been sacrificed in many instances. Aesthetic appeal can be reduced when attention turns to functionalism, as in the case of vandalism reduction. Materials selection based on durability alone may or may not provide the desired aesthetic qualities. Creative departments have devised strategies such as "adopt a park" in trying to adhere to previous maintenance standards while being called upon to cut staff and operation expenses.

Decisions must be made by corporate boards and public commissions so that the mission primary to existence is carefully detailed and known throughout the organization. Such scrutiny can produce benefits; the clear delineation of a mission statement serves as a viable starting point when objectives are being formulated within the organization. Employees are able to understand how their tasks contribute to the agency mission.

When the mission statement has been made final, and management is assured that it accurately describes the purpose of the agency (and it would be wise to have the statement or statements printed and available for all employees), each unit or functional area should review existing objectives or develop new ones. Objectives are the focal points that allow the mission statement to be translated into program service. Each unit, such as parks, special events, athletics, etc., should reach consensus on the objectives that will guide its efforts. The next step is to analyze each position within the department to pinpoint the major impact areas. Alexander (1980:43) defines "impact areas" as the general categories of accountability for each job. Simply put, they are the key result areas or the areas of one's job having high priority. Impact areas can be discerned by answering the question, "What aspects of my job are likely to result in praise or recognition if I perform them properly?" Employees in private industry would likely list sales volume, production costs, and quality of output as impact areas; those in leisure-service profession might view perceived program quality, development of novel activities, and effective documentation as critical impact areas.

The listing of job impact areas should be a joint effort between supervisor and subordinate (Dunnette 1966; Yoder and Heneman 1974). The typical job description should provide many of these impact areas, although often such descriptions do not accurately reflect the current demands of a particular position, and the aforementioned process of reviewing the agency mission statement and accompanying objectives may render some job descriptions unsuitable.

Once impact areas have been agreed upon, a listing of priorities should occur. Begin with those areas essential to the position. Alexander (1980:45) has suggested that a numerical weight or percentage of the total responsibilities be assigned to each impact area. For example, the recreation supervisor and the community center director may agree that the direct supervision of the facility is the most important impact area and that it represents approximately 40 percent of total job demands. If supervisors and supervisees experience initial difficulty in prioritizing the impact areas, a rating scale can be employed (1 representing the lowest priority, 10 the highest, for example) and mean scores obtained. Impact areas can then easily be ranked.

The next step in the process is determining measures of competent performance for each of the impact areas. Administrators in the human services are keenly aware that this task is not an easy one. Rockwood (1982:294) comments on the lack of pertinent criteria used when performance is measured: "In spite of pleas for objectivity in performance evaluations, there is no question but what personal, informal, and unarticulated criteria frequently are the real basis on which ratings are made rather than the technicality of how well an individual meets job descriptions."

It must be kept in mind that the more objective the measure, the better. Careful thought, discussion, and perhaps future modification will lead to the establishment of effective performance measures. It is also possible to prioritize performance measures, as was suggested earlier for impact areas. In the example used earlier, direct supervision was given as a critical impact area for the center director. Competency measures of "good" supervision might be:

1. A cost-effectiveness ratio between staff required and hours open or numbers served
2. Accident statistics showing low rates per participant
3. Praise or a lack of complaints by attenders or parents of attenders.

Rather than focusing on a negative standard (lack of complaints, for example), managers may find it helpful to develop measures of performance oriented toward positive situations. Keeping letters from pleased participants or noting written comments that praise staff on standard evaluation forms is useful in creating a positive momentum. Certainly time will be consumed in this phase of devising an effective performance evaluation system, but, over time, reliable measures of competency will replace subjective criteria.

A case study

A pilot test was conducted to determine how a group of recreation center directors perceived the impact or key result areas of their jobs, and if they were able to suggest measures of their performance which could be used for evaluation purposes. The intent was not to develop a definitive list of key impact areas or performance measures not applicable to all center directors, but to analyze the process of creating the evaluation paradigm presented earlier. Impact areas are often situationally specific, for some of the reasons indicated previously. Readers are cautioned to examine the evaluation process discussed for possible adaptation rather than focusing on the "findings" reported. Current research underway by the author, and future studies by other investigators interested in personnel evaluation, should provide desired generalizability.

Six recreation center directors (each had primary responsibility for the planning, supervision, and evaluation of activities at a year-round facility) were surveyed in a large urban park, recreation, and community-services department in the Northeast. Participants were asked whether their responsibilities had changed during recent months, and each rated a list of job impact areas by assigning them "high," "medium," or "low" priority. To determine if the directors were able to suggest performance measures, a list of five predetermined job tasks was given them, and they were asked to respond in open-ended fashion how each task could be measured.

The mission of the department consisted of the provision of leisure activities for all persons within the geographic boundaries of the city, and included conducting many large special events, which drew regional participation. Center directors were charged with establishing a year-round program for adults and children in their community with the guidance of their center council.

All directors had supervisory responsibilities (the mean number of employees supervised was 14.8, full- and part-time), and opinion was split as to whether the elements of their jobs had changed recently. Half indicated that their jobs had not been markedly altered, while the other half perceived a greater emphasis on administrative functions and a lessening of their responsibilities in the program leadership role. Publicity, paperwork, and improving community relationships were noted as areas of increased concern.

A list of twenty-four job impact areas was compiled from available job descriptions and previous discussion with staff. Supervisors rated each of the impact areas by assigning them a high priority (3), a medium priority (2), or a low priority (1). Table 1 shows the results. Six items received a perfect mean score of 3.0 and were considered high-priority impact areas: organizing activities, seasonal planning, supervising staff, reporting and record keeping, scheduling, and conducting staff meetings. Participants were not asked to indicate any further type of weighting system, such as the percent of their total responsibility represented by each area; however, given the unanimity expressed it is logical to assume that this group of center directors felt that the six areas should weigh heavily in their performance evaluation.

At the opposite end of the range was the list of seven items that received ratings below 2.0 and constituted the low-priority impact areas. Center directors viewed training volunteers, coaching sports, serving as a club advisor, collecting fees (this was a centralized process in this organization), officiating, maintenance, and leadership in crafts, ceramics, table games, and senior citizen activities as being less critical in terms of their total job performance.

The final part of the survey sought the respondents' views on how performance might be measured effectively. If job evaluation is to be successful, not only must there be agreement as to what the key impact or result areas are, but the methods or means of evaluation must be established also. The goal should be to minimize subjective elements and move toward objective standards. This task proved the most difficult of all the survey items for the directors questioned.

Five job result areas were listed, and responses as to how the area could be measured were given in open-ended fashion. The five areas were general building supervision, seasonal planning of programs, supervision of full-time and part-time staff, supervision of equipment and supplies, and activity leadership. The responses indicated that there appears to be a bias in favor of the easily quantifiable (in, for example attendance figures or numbers of complaints) and that further development of measures of quality (program effectiveness or changed behavior of clients) is needed. In addition, job inputs were frequently mentioned (Did staff have the proper training? Were supplies on hand?) whereas the evaluation of center directors most often focuses on outputs—quality instruction or the ability to handle emergencies, for example. Performance measures suggested for general building supervision included visual inspection of the building, the visibility and positioning of the supervisor, the amount of damage to the building, and the number of complaints received. In terms of measurability, problems emerged with

Table 1. Ranking of job impact areas—center directors.

Impact areas	Mean rating*
Plan and organize activities	3.0
Plan seasonal programs	3.0
Assign and supervise staff	3.0
Keep daily records, reports	3.0
Schedule activities, rooms at center	3.0
Conduct staff meetings	3.0
Control equipment and supplies	2.8
Promote programs, public relations	2.6
Perform emergency first aid	2.6
Solve complaints from public	2.6
Generally supervise building	2.2
Organize the advisory committee	2.2
Prepare the budget for the facility	2.2
Attend community and school meetings	2.2
Assign and supervise volunteers	2.0
Train staff	2.0
Participate in long-range planning	2.0
Train volunteers	1.8
Coach team sports and games	1.8
Advisor to clubs	1.8
Collect and account for fees	1.8
Provide leadership in areas of crafts, table games, senior activities	1.6
Officiate team sports	1.6
Perform regular maintenance	1.2

* High priority = 3.0
  Medium priority = 2.0
  Low priority = 1.0

this group of indicators. The elements of the visual inspection should be articulated. Building damage might indicate heavy usage, or vandalism by non-users when staff are not on duty. Even the center director's visibility can create problems in measuring effectiveness. If the supervisor drops by and does not find the center director at his or her proper "station," the reason may be legitimate; the director may be responding to a problem elsewhere or performing some type of community involvement such as attending a neighborhood meeting.

In terms of activity leadership the measures recommended were attendance figures, the presence of materials and equipment, the use of publicity in advertising the program, and written evaluations by participants. The last measure is most suited to evaluating outputs, provided that the objectives of the program are made known initially and used as criteria during the final assessment. The other three areas (seasonal planning, supervision of staff, and equipment supervision) yielded responses similar to those areas above. Most respondents expressed their difficulty in suggesting measures that would be applicable all of the time, that incorporated external factors which should be considered, and that were sensitive to degrees of performance.

It is suggested that supervisors and subordinates meet and attempt to develop appropriate measures, which will undoubtedly be refined over time. Modification is inherent in this process of analyzing departmental objectives, job impact or result areas, and the measures to be used in defining competent performance; the interchange between supervisors and subordinates will be a positive force in creating a better understanding of the way each job contributes to the success of the organization. As employees recognize the key elements of their position and how their performance will be measured, fewer energies will need to be wasted on non-critical areas.

Summary

The preceding paragraphs have discussed a current organizational climate that indicates a need for improved performance appraisal, particularly for leisure-service agencies within the public sector, so vulnerable to the budget axe in uncertain economic times. The strengths and weaknesses of various assessment systems, such as management by objectives, have been discussed, and a process has been advocated composed of a careful analysis of the organizational mission statement and accompanying objectives, a detailing of the key result or impact areas of each position, and the establishment of appropriate performance measures for the essential impact areas.

By undergoing the proposed evaluation process, supervisory and subordinate personnel should be able to approach a consensus as to what the key elements of each position are and how competent performance can be measured. Such analysis can only assist the agency in more clearly defining or redefining its purpose and providing its employees with needed direction regarding job performance.

References

Alexander, J. 1980. Making managers accountable: Develop objective performance standards. *Management Review*, December, 43-46.

Dunnette, M.D. 1966. *Observing and recording job behavior*. Belmont, Calif.: Wadsworth. Cited in D. Berryman. 1980. Evaluating professional personnel. In *Personnel management in recreation and leisure services*, ed. A. Grossman. South Plainfield, N.J.: Groupwork Today.

Edginton, C., and J. Williams. 1978. *Productive management of leisure service organizations: A behavioral approach.* New York: John Wiley and Sons.

Rockwood, L. 1982. *Public parks and recreation administration: Behavior and dynamics*. Salt Lake City: Brighton Publishing Co.

Rodney, L., and R. Toalson. 1981. *Administration of recreation, parks, and leisure services*. New York: John Wiley and Sons.

Spooner, P., and M. Johnson. 1980. Managers in the future: How will they be judged? *Management Review*, December, 8-17.

Yoder, D., and H.G. Heneman, Jr., eds. 1974. *ASPA handbook of personnel and industrial relations*, vol. 1, *Staffing policies and strategies*. Washington, D.C.: Bureau of National Affairs. Cited in D. Berryman. 1980. Evaluating professional personnel. In *Personnel management in recreation and leisure services*, ed. A. Grossman. South Plainfield, N.J.: Groupwork Today.

Productivity through Worker Incentive and Satisfaction

Daniel G. Hobbs

Welcome to Rockville, Maryland, a community of 50,000 people. Located 12 miles (19.2 kilometers) northwest of Washington, D.C., Rockville also serves as the county seat for Montgomery County, a rapidly urbanizing suburb of the nation's capital. The city of Rockville employs 350 people in 7 departments. Forty percent of these employees are formally unionized, represented by the American Federation of State, County and Municipal Employees. These employees perform parks maintenance and public works activities.

Beginning in late 1976, the Rockville city government initiated a productivity program called the "Worker Incentive and Satisfaction Program" (WISP). This title was used for several reasons. The goal of the program was job enrichment and job satisfaction—which would increase productivity in turn. Also, the union had already demonstrated its antagonism toward the term "productivity." Previously, when management had brought up productivity during a collective bargaining session, union officials nearly walked out in protest. Therefore, an acceptable program title was critical both in gaining union support and in communicating the city's intention to work with *all* employees—unionized, middle management, and senior management.

One year later, the project showed a direct and indirect cost saving of $27,173. Procedures and morale had improved, and the need for productivity within the organization was better appreciated. The key ingredient in the program's success was the *consultation* with the supervisors and employees and *their involvement* in

This article first appeared in TRENDS, vol. 18, no. 2, 1981. TRENDS is cooperatively produced by the National Park Service and the National Recreation and Park Association.

both the selection and execution of projects. Five measures were used to determine the effectiveness of the program:

Direct cost savings

Indirect cost savings

Improved procedures

Improved morale or a better management-labor relationship

Consciousness raising of supervisors and employees regarding the need for improved productivity and efficiency (which could generate other opportunities for savings).

Program origins

A productivity program does not just spring up out of the ground. It requires careful planning, discussion, and consultation. The seed must be sown long before productivity blossoms. For example, consider the environment and circumstances from which the Rockville program evolved.

In 1974 the city began its first comprehensive training program of all 89 supervisory personnel. The program was funded with a $5,000 federal Intergovernmental Personnel Act grant. The National Training and Development Service for State and Local Government (NTDS) helped the 89 city supervisors identify their needs and develop their own training agenda.

The following year, to avert a strike by the city's union employees, Rockville established cost savings task forces representing both labor and management. The task forces were charged with finding hard savings that would be shared on a 50-50 cash basis with the union employees. Some $6,200 in savings was identified, and a modest amount of $23.30 given to each employee.

Spurred on by this success, the city engaged NTDS in September 1976 to facilitate a Worker Incentive and Satisfaction Program aimed at improving organizational productivity. This program was funded with $4,500 from the state of Maryland under the federal Intergovernmental Personnel Act.

And so began the Rockville productivity program.

What happened?

In September 1976, a task force of 15 employees and supervisors from the Public Works Department and the Recreation and Parks Department met to discuss target opportunities for increased productivity. At the onset, it was anticipated that the task force would address only 3 or 4 target items. By the time the program was completed, however, the task force had successfully addressed 12 of the issues previously identified as target opportunities. Let's examine 2 of the most important ones: reducing absenteeism and the 4-day work week.

Reducing absenteeism

Employee absenteeism and sick leave abuse concern most organizations, and Rockville was no exception. A special task force of management and union personnel reviewed this problem area and offered many suggestions. The city followed through on the following items.

The city's policy of requiring a doctor's certificate to document illness was reaffirmed.

Superintendents reviewed day-to-day work procedures to ensure consistency in all divisions. These procedures then were discussed with all employees.

Demotion within grade for leave abuse was discussed with union representatives and will be considered as a disciplinary option in the future.

The personnel director made available to the employees a list of available counseling resources ranging from psychiatric to marital counseling.

The task force's efforts, combined with the serious discussions of leave abuse during the last 2 years of union negotiations, have reduced sick leave usage and absenteeism by blue-collar workers 23.5 percent. This translates into 4,064 man-hours saved for $21,873 in productivity savings.

Experimental four-day work week

In the motor vehicle maintenance shop, Rockville began an *experimental* 4-day work week with 10-hour days to provide quicker and better servicing of the city's 195 vehicles.

Data collected during the first year of the experiment showed a productivity increase of 22.5 percent in the number of units serviced and a reduction of more than $3,000 in overtime costs. The new 4-day schedule also gave the division an opportunity to conduct in-house training programs for the mechanics. Employee morale significantly increased within the division, as measured by survey research. Prior to the experiment, complaints from departments about the speed of vehicle service were averaging between two and three per week. These complaints were reduced to less than one per month during the experiment.

An interesting footnote to this productivity breakthrough is that the initial concept was pushed by a middle manager in the Public Works Department who has the reputation of being a no-nonsense, by-the-book supervisor. It was an idea that I, as assistant city manager, was not very interested in originally. But the productivity program gave this manager the chance to try out some of his ideas based on what he knew to be the needs of his division. And they worked.

Union perspective

The president of American Federation of State, County and Municipal Employees (AFSCME) Local #1453, who represented Rockville's unionized employees on the productivity task force, made these comments about the program:

Several of the union members, stewards, and myself sat in on groups that were looking for ways to save money for the city in order to reach a better negotiated settlement than what the city said it could afford.

We get very suspicious whenever management uses the term "productivity" because we think that what that can mean is more work and less pay. . . . There is just so much work a man can do in any one day. The nature of our work in the public works and recreation departments lends itself to limitations as to how much the human body can physically do in a given time.

The whole program was supposed to involve more than just "productivity." It was supposed to deal with workers and their problems. Problems and situations that could be improved while helping the city save money. The men could benefit as a result of their efforts. . . . We think we have some pretty good ideas on where money can be saved and how the job could be done better with the skilled employees that we have.

I would like to point out that it is very important in this type of a program to involve the men and that both the men and the city benefit as a result of this effort. I don't think you can really do anything that will last very long unless the men are involved and know the reasons behind some of the changes that are made. If nothing else, you'd be surprised at how these sessions open up more communication between the union and management.

Based on what I have observed in the program, and based on what my fellow workers told me about the program, it has shown some success because the men participated in it and we would like to see the program extended.

Management perspective

The director of Recreation and Parks, who was also involved in the program, offered these views:

I was very anxious to explore the possibilities of the productivity program. This opportunity forced me to think of inefficient areas that existed in our department that needed help.

Our Park Maintenance Division is responsible for parks, city buildings, rights-of-way, street trees, bikeways, and stream valley maintenance. These are important services to the community. But we were asked to take on increased responsibility without adding manpower. The only answer was to improve our productivity. The following are some examples of how we have reached our goal of higher productivity at a lower cost.

1. The department purchased more mowing equipment and virtually eliminated trimming. This equipment was used on our rights-of-way and enabled our crews to mow more areas and to do the job better.
2. The department used part-time summer help for $2.50 per hour, assigned to specific park sites. This has cut the cost per site and improved appearance. For example, one summer employee now performs full-time the routine summer maintenance on the City Hall grounds whereas previously a crew of 6 maintained the area once a week.
3. Regular meetings between our park superintendent and the 6 foremen have improved worker/management relations so that problems can be noted and discussed before their effects become critical. This has helped uplift morale.

Still other benefits are occurring and we believe the program will help the department keep pace with the future.

Phase two

Based upon the initial success of the productivity program, Rockville decided in June 1978 to try the same consultative approach with the rest of its work force, especially the nonunionized employees. This time, instead of meeting with a task force designed to represent the employees, management decided to meet with *all the employees* to describe the program and directly solicit productivity ideas and suggestions.

Four months into phase 2, nine seminars attended by more than 230 employees had been held. Approximately 25-30 employees from different departments attended each session. Each work group viewed a 14-minute slide show describing the initial productivity program, then discussed a printed handout on the current program's objectives, criteria, and ground rules. This handout consisted of the following:

I.   Objectives of Productivity 2
     A. Direct cost savings (hard cash)
     B. Indirect cost savings
     C. Improved procedures
     D. Improved morale (includes better working conditions)
     E. Awareness of need for additional productivity and efficiency
II. Criteria and ground rules
     A. All suggestions reviewed with respective department head or supervisor based on:
        1. Feasibility

    2. Cost trade-offs (for example, examination of any additional capital investment; additional personnel costs, and so forth)

    3. Acceptance by both labor and management

  B. No reduction in service quantity or quality

  C. Hard savings are important (suggestion should generate actual cash)

Review process   Under "Criteria and Ground Rules," it is important to note that management was committed to reviewing all suggestions with the appropriate department head or supervisor. It was considered critical not to bypass the supervisory and departmental personnel. These people are paid to supervise, to manage, to get the job done. Top management did not want to be viewed as undercutting their role.

Feasibility and cost trade-offs   The feasibility of a suggestion is examined to determine whether it really can be implemented, or whether it is just a crazy idea.

    There were some employee suggestions made to the effect that "if only I could hire two more people, I could save the city $7,000 a year." This necessitated a review of the cost trade-offs. What does it cost to hire two people, with fringe benefits, with additional equipment, and so forth? Does the city make money or lose money? What is the pay-back on the city's investment?

Acceptance by labor and management   In requiring that a productivity idea be acceptable to both labor and management, management demonstrated explicitly that the goal of the program was to get things done, to solve problems. Management did not want to create more problems through these suggestions—and certainly did not want to aggravate or anger a group of employees.

    If someone came up with a brilliant idea that was unacceptable to labor or to management, that idea would be tabled, no ifs, ands, or buts about it.

No reduction in service   The program mandate of no reduction in service quantity or quality placed an additional constraint on the employees' productivity suggestions. But again, this constraint was in the open for everyone to see.

    For example, the city could save money by cutting grass in the parks once every 10 days instead of once every 5 days. However, that definitely would reduce the service quality that has been established through the annual program budget.

    The city also could save significant dollars if the twice-a-week backyard refuse collection service were changed to once-a-week curbside pickup. However, that would deviate from a deliberate city policy decision. Therefore, such a suggestion would not fall within the scope of this program.

In discussing these criteria and ground rules with the employees, no negative attitudes were expressed toward the constraints put on the program. Probably this was because our approach was extremely forthright and everyone understood the reasoning behind the constraints. In other words, everyone knew the rules of the game going into it. The importance of that cannot be overstated.

Employee reaction   What resulted from this approach? There was terrific feedback from the employees! They all appreciated having the opportunity to sit down with top management to discuss their ideas. It was a chance to get the "if only the city would" feeling out of everyone's system. The 9 sessions generated 249 suggestions, with little duplication.

Not only were the sessions great opportunities to elicit solid productivity ideas from the employees, they also provided a chance for me, as assistant city manager, to discuss city policy with the employees. One of the basic ground rules that I followed in these sessions was listing every idea that employees wished to bring up. There were no names attached to any of the suggestions. When particular items came up which represented an opportunity to comment on city policy or to provide some background, I did so. I tried to be as objective as possible. Given some of the suggestions and the context in which they were delivered, it was sometimes difficult not to become defensive or to show irritation. I felt it was critical to be receptive to each idea; yet, I had to correct misstatements or provide additional factual background when it seemed appropriate. Here is an example of how this worked.

One item that continually arose was the need for more employee space. For years city employees have worked in cramped office conditions; presently they are scattered at six different sites. Thus, when the productivity suggestion was made that the city could save money and increase employee efficiency by providing reasonable office space in one location, I could point out that the city was indeed funding an addition to the City Hall. This addition will consolidate all city offices into one location and provide reasonable office space. This information was appreciated by many of the employees who had not been aware of it.

In summary, the information exchange process that resulted from the productivity discussion presented a set of payoffs that, alone, contributed to better employee morale.

There were two possible dangers inherent in this approach of meeting with employees. First, it is easy for this type of meeting to degenerate into a gripe session. There was a tendency for this to happen when many of the employees in a work session were from the same department. Secondly, there was the possibility of a "planted agenda," where several employees might get together and push for the same item, that item being something of particular interest to them. However, the payoffs derived from these meetings with the employees were far greater than these potential drawbacks.

How productivity items were analyzed   The productivity suggestions made by the employees were checked out by administrative interns in the city manager's office. These interns are graduate students at area universities who are enrolled in masters of public administration programs and have an interest in becoming municipal managers. For $3.75 an hour, they performed mini cost/benefit analyses of each suggestion under the supervision of the assistant city manager.

The interns attended the sessions with the employees so that they would understand the context in which the various suggestions were made. Work meetings were held with the interns to make assignments and to refer them to the appropriate people for checking out each suggestion. These meetings also helped the interns acquire a managerial perspective on these issues.

These young professionals performed a real service for the organization because they approached each job with an energy and enthusiasm seldom found in someone who has been around awhile. Although management retained final review over all recommendations that were made, the graduate students did such a good job on the mini cost/benefit analyses that few recommendations were overruled.

A breakdown of the 109 analyses made within 6 months of program initiation showed that the city was able to implement quickly about 25 percent of the productivity suggestions; management already was taking action on another 25 percent of the items; and about 35 percent of the suggestions were rejected. The other productivity suggestions remained under consideration.

Figure 1 shows some of the productivity ideas generated by the employees during the work sessions and the type of payoff projected for the city by each idea.

The inside scoop—from the assistant city manager
Three crucial elements of the Rockville productivity story warrant explicit explanation.

1. *Productivity, in the Rockville fashion, is a real opportunity to communicate with employees on a practical level about their work situation.* This is not a forced "organizational develop-

	Direct cost	Indirect cost	Proce-dures	Morale
Implemented				
Graphics form revision	X	X	X	
Employee handbook update			X	X
Supervisory training program			X	X
Resolution of refuse collection problems			X	X
a. Cans not accessible				
b. Residents put some refuse at curb, some at house				
c. Commercial grass cutting				
Future implementation				
Train secretaries in typewriter care	Maybe		X	X
Orientation on purchasing forms		Maybe	X	X
Senior staff meet with purchasing agent			X	X
Update evaluation form			X	X
Let employees contribute to equipment specs			X	X
Salespeople discuss products with employees			X	X
Already being done				
Floating secretary			X	
Better janitorial service				X
Wheelchair access at Community Resources			X	
Map showing city buildings			X	
Examine quantity of recreation flyers	X	X		
Personnel Procedures Manual update			X	X

Figure 1. Employee-generated productivity ideas and projected payoffs.

ment" type of discussion. Rather, it is a nitty-gritty, down-to-earth discussion about the day-to-day activities of the employees and about how money could be saved by people working smarter, if not harder. From my own experience in these discussions, I state flatly and unequivocally that you, as a manager or a supervisor, will come away with more insight about the job that is going on out there—no matter how many years you have been working with a particular division or work unit.

2.   *The Rockville process provides an opportunity for managers at all levels to try some things that ordinarily might be a little*

risky. This is your chance to experiment. You can try out some things ordinarily not permitted without numerous clearances from above. Without being too cynical, this means you can roll out the agenda you have been saving for years. You can now institute that change, try out that new approach to the work activity that was previously considered a little bit risky—all by calling it a *productivity experiment.* The employees, likewise, may take this advantage to suggest that the organization try out some things that heretofore may have been looked upon with a jaundiced eye. That brings us to the next point.

3. *Be comfortable that you are not giving the shop away and you will not give the shop away.* Top management always retains at least a veto over what items the organization will or will not try. You always control the agenda, and you are in the driver's seat as the decisionmaker for the organization. Consultation with the employees in no way diminishes the final decisionmaking authority that management *can and should retain at all times.*

We really did not know the results of the productivity effort until near the end when we tallied up the numbers. You cannot assess the situation properly until there has been enough time and experience for the numbers to come in. Frankly, we were surprised at our success. Most of the productivity literature indicates that this is a fairly common experience in productivity efforts. The Rockville productivity story is not a story of one success after another. It is rather a story of an array of activities, involving the employees, set into motion under the umbrella of productivity.

A special newsletter of the National League of Cities on productivity set realistic expectations for these efforts nationwide:

Interestingly, few dramatic successes are claimed to result from productivity programs. On the other hand, even failures seem to have some positive results. Most efforts show savings or at least leveling off of expenditures. Improved management and decision-making systems frequently are cited as outcomes. Approaching a productivity program as a panacea is bound to be a disillusioning experience. Yet a well-managed productivity program, which includes a measurement system, appears to be one of the most hopeful ways of dealing with the demands for high quality service at low cost that are placed on local governments today.

The Rockville productivity program had modest results. The hard dollars, the direct savings, were not that big. The Rockville program is not a story about New York City saving $7 million as a result of a time/motion study or a significant technological breakthrough. However, *this modest success is the strength of the Rockville productivity program for most organizations,* especially smaller organizations. These organizations can relate to Rockville's size and to Rockville's process; they will not be intimidated by this kind of "productivity." Therefore, they are more likely to try the productivity process out for their own situation.

That is why the real strength of the Rockville productivity story is the *process*. Anyone can use this approach, which is open-ended and very simple. Your needs and opportunities will be just that, yours, not Rockville's. You can't imitate our productivity items, but you can imitate our process.

What is different about the Rockville program?

In the past decade, cities and counties have utilized a variety of methods to improve productivity. The *Guide to Management Improvement Projects*, prepared by the International City Management Association, lists a number of productivity improvements that have been tried across the country.

Many of these projects are applications of technology; for example, data processing, mechanized refuse collection, solid waste recycling, new paving materials, and modifications to fire-fighting vehicles. Other productivity improvements have involved employee incentives, training programs, work scheduling, performance auditing, and industrial engineering. Rockville's productivity program differed from these efforts in other cities in several ways:

1. The program was comprehensive. Phase 2 covered *all* city departments, rather than concentrating on one aspect of city services.
2. Employees were the source of productivity ideas. Rockville's program was built on the philosophy that employees are the "experts" in their work situations. Given the opportunity, workers can develop their own ideas for productivity improvements and will, therefore, be receptive to the ensuing changes.
3. The program brought employees and management together in an atmosphere of free and open discussion.

Why productivity makes sense

Whether or not the Rockville productivity process is right for you and your organization, productivity does make good fiscal sense. We all are looking for ways to save dollars. In this post–Proposition 13 era, productivity may be a necessity rather than a luxury.

Productivity also makes good political sense. Elected officials like it, and it sells well to the public. Productivity by means of the Rockville process can and should improve labor-management relations. Those of us in municipal managerial positions tend to take for granted our opportunity to influence our own job situations, city policy, and the allocations of resources among community activities. Other people are no different; they, too, like to have some say over their jobs. They, too, appreciate the opportunity to express their ideas about how their job could be made easier, more productive, or less wasteful. These kinds of productivity discussions with the employees can have big payoffs for the agencies.

Through Rockville's productivity program, dollars were saved for the city. Improved procedures and better morale resulted. From our perspective, inside the project, it seems like a modest success. Maybe, though, the project assumes even more significance, if we can share the lessons that we learned from this process with you.

PART 3

Budgeting and Financial Strategies

Fund Accounting: A Standard Accounting Technique

J. Robert Rossman

Fund accounting is a standard accounting technique used by governments. Generally accepted accounting principles (GAAP) as specified by the National Council on Governmental Accounting have directed that government resources are to be allocated to and accounted for in separate funds according to the purposes the resources serve and the legal restrictions on their use.

Most accounting activity in government has centered around the preparation of score-keeping fund statements which have reported the amount budgeted, the amount disbursed to date, and the balance remaining in each line item of a fund. These reports have been prepared for groups external to the organization such as commissions, boards, the public, etc., to verify fiscal responsibility and to verify that dollars have been disbursed for their legal purposes.

As currently practiced, fund accounting is generally an externally oriented accounting system with little benefit for internal management decisions. This article will discuss the need for and benefit of an internally oriented management accounting system and discuss how the concept of fund accounting can be used in an expanded way to provide useful management accounting information.

Management accounting

The goal of management accounting is to prepare financial data which are useful to management in directing the organization toward its social and programmatic goals. Although externally oriented financial accounting practices are well defined and require strict adherence to accepted conventions, this is not the case for in-

*Management Strategy*Reprinted with permission from *Management Strategy*, vol. 8, no. 4, Winter 1984. Management Learning Laboratories, Champaign, Illinois.

ternally oriented management accounting. In developing a management accounting system, managers are free to make and enforce whatever rules and definitions they find most useful in developing accounting information.[1] The focus in management accounting is on developing information that is useful within the agency for discharging the management function rather than conforming to generally accepted accounting principles. Managers need accounting information for a variety of reasons, including planning, pricing, measuring performance, decision-making and monitoring decisions made. Different information is usually needed for each of these purposes, so management accounting information must often be assembled in several different ways.

A management accounting system is made up of two functions—cost accounting and responsibility accounting. Each function is dependent on the other and essentially, they are reinterpretations of the same accounting information. The objective of cost accounting is to identify all costs of service production and to allocate those costs to all service outputs. With the introduction of computerized accounting procedures, many agencies have implemented extensive cost-tracking systems. This is an important step in developing cost accounting. However, there is usually great reluctance to complete this cost allocation process and track overhead or burden costs. Managers are often uncomfortable that some costs cannot be scientifically determined and allocated. Consequently, they continue to have unassigned overhead categories such as: administration, office support, etc. To have an accurate management accounting system, managers must make ambiguous allocation decisions on these types of items. The objective of cost accounting is not to arrive at an absolutely correct allocation, but to assign to all service outputs a "fair share" of overhead and burden costs. This can be done.

There are several methods for helping managers make these allocations and each has a differing degree of accuracy. For example, if one has identified ten service outputs of an organization and assumes the chief executive contributes equally to each, one tenth of the chief executive's salary could be allocated to each. This may be a crude, but adequate approximation of the actual situation. If more accuracy is required, a time budget analysis of the chief executive's work schedule could be completed. Results of this analysis could be used to establish varying percentages of the executive's salary to be charged to outputs according to actual percentages of time spent dealing with each output. Many other methods for making cost allocation decisions exist. However, one must always consider whether the cost of increasing accuracy makes a real or practical difference in view of the purpose for which the data will be used. In any case, there is always a good deal of professional judgment involved in cost allocation decisions. However, managers closest to operations are usually best qualified to make these estimates. Once an allocation method has been determined, it should be consistently applied for several accounting periods so that the data developed can be reliably compared from period to period.

The goal of responsibility accounting is to assign identified costs to responsibility centers rather than service outputs. Cost data generated in the cost accounting procedure are used to assign to responsibility centers the costs incurred by them. A responsibility center is a subunit in an organization which is headed by a manager who is responsible for performing some line function, i.e., the responsibility center's output. In producing its output, a responsibility center uses inputs from the organization which are costs for the organization. The objective, then, of responsibility accounting is to assign to responsibility centers the costs they incur in producing their output for a specific time period. To be truly accurate, all expenses of the organization must be allocated as costs to some service output and each service output must be assigned to a responsibility center.

Designing responsibility centers is a major management decision and in making these decisions, several factors should be considered. First, a manager of a responsibility center must truly have managerial control over a substantial portion of the costs incurred by the center. Every center will have controllable and noncontrollable costs. However, responsibility centers must be designed so that managers can control their destiny and not simply oversee the disbursement of noncontrollable costs. Second, the number of centers should be kept at a manageable level. The creation of too many centers will fragment accounting data until it no longer yields useful information. Developing a hierarchy of responsibility centers is preferable to the creation of a large number of centers. Third, costs must be reported on a timely basis and in a manner which facilitates managerial performance. Managerial accounting data need to be reported in time for managers to take warranted action. The data must also provide timely feedback on the results of managerial action and be designed to reveal the effects of a manager's decision-making on progress in achieving the organization's goals. Designing responsibility centers is as important to the success of a management accounting system as good cost allocation procedures. Responsibility centers should be carefully designed with detailed attention given to the number, size, and make-up of the centers and the reporting procedures to be used in the system.

A properly designed management accounting system records, classifies and reports the costs of agency operations in ways that reflect a manager's progress toward meeting the agency's goals. The only accounting convention applicable to their development is that the data created are useful to the ongoing management of the organization. Fund accounting, which is a standard accounting procedure in government, can be used in an expanded way to provide a management accounting system.

Fund accounting

Governmental accountants are specific in defining a fund: "A fund is defined as a fiscal and accounting entity with a self-balancing set of accounts recording cash and other financial resources, together with all related liabilities and residual equities or balances, and changes therein, which are segregated for the purpose of carrying on specific activities or attaining certain objectives in accordance with special regulations, restrictions, or limitations."[2]

A fund represents a specific phase of governmental operation which is handled as a separate fiscal entity. Usually, this segregation of funds is required by parties external to the organization through legal restrictions, regulations, or limitations on the use of the fund's resources. When used an an internal management accounting technique, resources are segregated into funds by managerial directive. This segregation permits more observation and control of an activity.

The steps necessary for implementing a management accounting system using funds are diagrammed in Figure 1. First, one begins with the accounting data in a line-item budget. Second, service outputs are identified, a fund is created for each, and all costs associated with producing the service output are allocated to the fund's expenses. Next, each fund is assigned the user fees and charges it generates, and finally, each fund is balanced with all other sources of revenue including tax dollars, donations, third party funding, etc. By definition, revenues and expenses in each fund must balance. When step two is completed, all of the organization's revenues will also be allocated and matched with service output costs.

The third step, then, involves assigning these funds to responsibility centers. With the data just developed, managers in charge of a responsibility center can determine the source of revenues and the source of costs that each of their service outputs are generating and

---

Line item budget
↓
Responsibility accounting

Responsibility centers are identified and
service output funds are assigned to them.
↓
Cost accounting

Service output funds are designated and
costs and revenues allocated to them.

Figure 1. Steps to implementing a management accounting system.

incurring. Accounting data presented in this manner will enable managers to observe and control the financial transactions of each service output more closely. Since, by definition, the expenses and revenues of a fund must balance, managers using the system are forced to work within an accounting structure which mandates accurate estimates of both expenses and revenues. Managers then, must truly manage both sides, i.e., expense and revenue, of their operation and exercise fiscal management through carefully planned resource allocations and volume estimates for each service output of the organization.

Although there are numerous strategies for developing a management accounting system for a public leisure service agency, the use of the fund concept is a logical extension of a well-accepted governmental accounting practice. How long and involved the development of such a system would be depends on the size of the agency, the degree of accuracy desired, and the size of the service output funds and responsibility centers one would identify for inclusion in the system. A strategy of beginning with crude overhead cost allocation procedures and increasing the accuracy of allocation procedures for an identifiable number of overhead costs each year would certainly be acceptable.

The goal of a management accounting system is not complete accuracy in an objective sense, but the development of accounting data which are useful to managers in making decisions which help them achieve the organization's goals. Elsewhere, it has been demonstrated that this type of data can be used for purposes such as helping managers achieve congruence between agency policy and fiscal performance, monitoring the percentages of a program's budget which are user fees versus tax subsidies, calculating user costs for a program, and drawing together diverse elements of an agency operation and isolating them for fiscal analysis.[3] Developing a management accounting system provides middle and lower level managers with an accounting system which will enable them to exercise more fiscal analysis and control over their areas of responsibility and provide them with a system for monitoring their progress in achieving the organization's goals. Expanding the use of fund accounting in the manner described is one strategy for implementing a management accounting system for public park and recreation agencies.

1. Anthony, R. N. *Management Accounting Principles* (rev. ed.). Homewood, IL: Irwin, 1970.
2. National Committee on Governmental Accounting. *Governmental Accounting, Auditing, and Financial Reporting.* Chicago, IL: Municipal Finance Officers Association of the United States and Canada, 1980.
3. Rossman, J. R. Fund Accounting. *Journal of Physical Education, Recreation & Dance.* April 1982, *53*: 4, pp. 54–55; 58.

Basic Budgeting and Financing of Parks and Recreation

Jerry D. Burnam

Financial planning and control are key aspects of the financial success of any commercial, private, not-for-profit, or governmental enterprise. Of all the techniques developed, many managers prefer one allowing for the integration of revenue and expense from a particular segment of the enterprise, especially if it can also account for changes in volume or participation levels in the segment under analysis. Such a technique should provide several alternative plans from among which one can be chosen which is compatible with the goals and objectives of the enterprise and can be monitored over its lifespan. This monitoring should reveal any discrepancies between the fiscal plan and actual events, providing a means of control, as the manager can take any action necessary to reach the planned outcome.

A planning and control technique stemming from economic theory, i.e., "contribution margin theory," incorporates all these attributes. Business and accounting have used this theory in their techniques of break-even analysis and cost-volume profit analysis. These two techniques have been used extensively in sales and production analysis. Regardless of the name, the theory concentrates on the isolation of a particular segment of an operation for a complete financial analysis of expected results. This technique means matching revenue derived from the operation of an enterprise, function, program, or activity with the direct and indirect expenses of that operation in order to discover the points at which revenue is less than expense (loss), equal to expense (break-even), and greater than expense (contribution margin). Normally "break-even" refers

Reprinted with permission from *Management Strategy*, vol. 7, no. 4, Winter 1983. Management Learning Laboratories, Champaign, Illinois.

Expense items	Row no.	Participation levels 5	10	15	20	21	25
Facility rental	1	$ 900.00	$ 900.00	$ 900.00	$ 900.00	$ 900.00	$ 900.00
Instruction	2	270.00	270.00	270.00	270.00	270.00	270.00
Advertising	3	58.00	58.00	58.00	58.00	58.00	58.00
Supervision	4	238.00	238.00	238.00	238.00	238.00	238.00
Fixed costs	5	1,466.00	1,466.00	1,466.00	1,466.00	1,466.00	1,466.00
Cost/participant	6	293.20	146.60	97.73	73.30	69.80	58.64
First aide	7	90.00	90.00	90.00	90.00	90.00	90.00
Second aide	8	—	—	90.00	90.00	90.00	90.00
Third aide	9	—	—	—	—	90.00	90.00
Total fixed costs	10	1,556.00	1,556.00	1,646.00	1,646.00	1,736.00	1,736.00
Cost/participant	11	311.20	155.60	109.73	82.30	82.66	69.44
Variable costs	12	70.00	140.00	210.00	280.00	294.00	350.00
TOTAL COSTS	13	$1,626.00	$1,696.00	$1,856.00	$1,926.00	$2,030.00	$2,086.00
Break-even		$ 325.20	$ 169.60	$ 123.73	$ 96.30	$ 96.66	$ 83.44

Table 1. Financial analysis for a ceramics class.

to sales volume at which the business neither makes a profit nor incurs a loss. It is the point at which sales revenue is exactly equal to all direct and indirect expenses. Similarly, if all expenses are included in the analysis, the contribution margin becomes the true profit of net income. The picture can change if some or all of the indirect expenses are not included in the analysis. The "break-even" point then becomes more theoretical than actual. The contribution margin would be just that, the dollar amount that could be applied to offset any indirect expenses not included or to offset the overhead (burden costs). Regardless of the accounting system used, any enterprise can modify this technique for its use.

Table 1 illustrates the technique. For our examples, we will select a single recreation activity contemplated by the City Recreation Department of Pleasantville, U.S.A. Under consideration is a class in ceramics, since classes in arts and crafts ranked high in a citywide survey. Such a class would fall within the mission of the department and meet at least one objective for the coming fiscal year. The next step is to formulate a series of questions that should reveal the expenses involved.

Question 1. Who in the department is the most logical person to take charge of the financial analysis of a class in ceramics? Logic dictated the recreation supervisor in the adult programs section because of a solid background in art.

Question 2. What facility has the necessary equipment and space for the class? None of the community centers or any other facility under the city's control had the space for ceramics. The local high school did have a ceramics lab, which could be rented at $30/hour and which would be available on Saturdays from 8:00 a.m. to noon.

Question 3. How much time is needed for a beginner in ceramics to reach the novice stage? Any class should be at least 3 hours long and at least 30 hours would be needed to bring a beginner to the novice stage. This is our first expense. A timeline of 3-hour classes for 10 weeks yields a total of 30 hours; 30 hours at $30/hour (from Question 2) would be $900 in rental expense. This expense is direct, because it would not have to be incurred unless the program were held; it is the same for the duration of the class and remains the same regardless of the number of participants. We recorded this $900 direct fixed expense in Row 1.

Question 4. Could a staff person teach this class, or is there some-one in the community who could be hired to do so? A retired art teacher with a specialty in ceramics was hired. The hourly pay rate agreed upon plus FICA contributions (Social Security), workmen's compensation, unemployment tax, and other fringe benefits total $9.00/hour, which times the 30-hour program yields $270.00 of direct expense. We recorded this expense in Row 2.

Question 5. What is the marketing and advertising plan for this class? Fifteen posters at $3.00 each, 500 flyers at 1¢ each, and one hour of clerical time to place press releases in the newspapers and announcements on cable TV at $8.00/hour yields a total of $58.00. These expenses are indirect and fixed, because they would still be incurred by the department whether or not the class was held and merely allocated to another program sponsored by the department, and because they normally involve support staff services that exist as expenses regardless of the programs sponsored. We entered this $58.00 expense in Row 3.

Question 6. Who will be responsible for the implementation, su-pervision, and evaluation of the ceramics class? The recreation su-pervisor is assigned those tasks. This person's total salary plus the value of all fringe benefits provided is $29,120 total, which divided by the 2,080 hours in a work year yields a $14.00/hour rate. An esti-mated 10 hours planning, 2 hours implementation, 3 hours supervi-sion, and 2 hours evaluation yield a total of 17 hours for an overall total of $238.00, an indirect fixed expense since the recreation super-visor would remain on the department's payroll even if the ceramics program were not held. We recorded this expense in Row 4.

Question 7. Will any of the balance of indirect expenses of the department be assigned to this class? These expenses, called overhead or burden costs, are necessary for the department's survival but are difficult to trace to any one segment. They include the director's salary, the operation of the business office, the central office utilities, general insurance, etc. It is currently not the policy of the department to allocate these overhead expenses to individual programs.

We recorded the total of all direct and indirect fixed costs in Row 5. We then calculated what the cost per participant would be by dividing the fixed cost by any given level of participation, completing Row 6 by dividing the $1,466 of fixed costs by the number of participants for each column. These dollar figures represent the actual cost of holding the program if the various participation levels were reached.

Question 8. What is the capacity of the facility being rented from the high school? The facility can accommodate a maximum of 30 people in one class.

Question 9. Can the instructor handle 30 participants and maintain a high-quality instructional program? It was decided that one instructional aide for every 10 or fewer participants was needed. High school art students could be hired as aides for $3.00/hour, a $90.00 expense per aide over the 30-hour course. This is a direct fixed cost, but it changes with each group of 10 or fewer participants. Changing fixed costs are expenses that increase with the addition of 2 or more participants. We labeled Row 7 "first aide" and recorded the expense. This remains a part of the total costs of the class from the lowest through the maximum participation levels.

We labeled Row 8 "second aide" and recorded the expenses. We *did not* record the expense of the second aide under columns 5 and 10 because the aide is not needed until the eleventh participant. Once we add this expense, it then exists as a part of the total program cost until the maximum participation level is reached.

We labeled Row 9 "third aide" and recorded the expenses. We then computed a total fixed cost for the program at the various participation levels. Beginning with the figure in Row 6, we then totaled the columns and recorded the numbers in Row 10, total fixed costs. We then calculated the cost/participant, Row 11.

Question 10. Are there any areas of expense that have been overlooked that would ensure the quality of the class? The local bookstore will provide instructional manuals for $4.00 each. The local art supply store agreed to supply at $8.00/person enough supplies for a beginning project. Additional supplies would be bought by the participant because remaining projects would be at his or her discretion. The local office supply store has nice certificates of completion for $2.00 each. Since we can purchase these items on an individual need basis and supply them to each participant, they are variable costs, fluctuating in direct proportion to each change in participation level. These expenses, when added together at any level of participation, plus the total fixed costs of the program at that level of participation, become the total costs of the class at that level. When one is completing a financial analysis of a program using this technique, all expenses must fall into one of the previously defined categories, depending on how each expense is treated.

A formula can now be given for this process using the various expense categories.

Direct fixed costs + Indirect fixed costs[1] +
Changing fixed costs + Variable costs = Program costs.

To complete Row 12, variable costs, we multiplied the $14.00 for supplies and manual by the various numbers of participants. Row 13, total costs, is the sum of total fixed costs in Row 10 and the variable costs in Row 12.

It is important to include all expenses of the program, including all direct and indirect fixed, all changing fixed, and all variable costs, in any financial analysis of a program to ensure that the true costs are known.

Revenue for this program is the next topic. Let's deal with direct revenue from the actual participants in the ceramics class. Revenue from participants can be calculated by two different methods. The first is by selecting a level of participation at which you would like to have participant revenue equal to the total costs for that level of participation, known as the break-even point. You calculate the total costs for that level and then figure cost/participant, which can be charged as tuition for the program. This method of revenue calculation is shown in Row 14. This row is another cost/participant calculation but we have labeled it "break-even." By dividing total costs, Row 13, by the column headings, we derived the balance needed for Row 14. The next participant to enroll in the program at that fee would generate a profit;[2] if your agency is not a commercial one this would be termed excess revenue over expenses or a contribution margin.

The second method of determining a participant fee is a market analysis to determine how much an individual would pay or has paid for similar programs. Once an educated guess has been made as to this figure, it is multiplied for various levels of participation and compared to the total costs for each level to determine loss, break-even, or profit.

Summary

The decision remains with you to convert your present accounting system to one that allows cost tracking by program and direct service centers for better financial decision making. It should always be remembered that financial decisions must be made to meet the objectives of your agency, which are reflected as dollar figures in your budget. It should also be remembered that the production of detailed accounting information has its own costs and only that information should be produced that will be useful in the decision-making process. This technique is intended for the use of dedicated managers who desire some help in better financial planning in the face of shrinking financial resources and who desire to provide greater opportunities for their clients.

1. To the extent that the agency desired them to be included; we deleted the overhead in our example.
2. A word of caution: Because of the nature and magnitude of changing fixed costs, this statement may not always be true. The next participant may *not* generate more revenue than expense, because it is possible to have more than one break-even point in any program and therefore more than one possibility of loss and profit.

Fees and Charges: Underutilized Revenues

James R. Waters

Directors of recreation and park departments throughout the country are faced with a common dilemma—declining budgets. Regardless of the cause of this problem—shrinking tax monies, unresponsive administration, or rebellious citizenry—each director is being forced to make decisions to either reduce the staff and services offered by the recreation department or to discover additional (or new) sources of revenue. Reducing staff and cutting back on services is repugnant to most directors and may not solve the problem—as services are cut back, the justification for the existence of the department may be jeopardized.

The alternative, seeking additional revenues or new revenues for departmental operation, is more viable, although not without its problems. Federal sources of grants and funds are disappearing, and generally the states have not stepped in to pick up this slack. Thus, the use of fees and charges (another source of additional revenue) for recreational activities and facilities is becoming more necessary.

Establishing a clear philosophy and policies

Whether instituting a new schedule of fees and charges or upgrading and increasing an existing fee schedule, it is necessary to first establish a clear departmental philosophy as related to the charging of fees. Questions related to who should pay these fees, how much of the program or facility costs will be covered by fees, whether certain groups should receive exemptions or special consideration, and which programs and facilities should be included in a fee schedule

Reprinted with permission from *Management Strategy*, vol. 6, no. 4, 1984. Management Learning Laboratories, Champaign, Illinois.

must all be answered beforehand. It is imperative that the governing body of the department—the legal board, the mayor, or the city/county commissioners—endorse this philosophy fully. Without this support, any operational policies constructed later would crumble when questioned.

The department must be ready to answer all of the arguments that will be broached by those opposed to a fee system. These arguments include the ideas that charging a fee is "double taxation," that fees may limit program participation to only those who can pay, that recreation is a "basic need" of everyone regardless of ability to pay, and that programs will be judged on the ability to generate income rather than their inherent worth. Each of these arguments can be countered, but the director should do his or her homework beforehand so as to not appear unprepared when confronted.

Specific policies must then be developed which will guide the actual operational procedures to be used by the department. Policies regarding minimum and maximum numbers of participants, percentages of costs to be used in calculation of the fees, fee schedule approval, fee waiver, and use of part-time instructors must be developed. As is the case with the departmental philosophy, it is very important that these policies be written in order to deal with later questions. From these policies, operating procedures can be formulated for the department. These procedures should include the method used to calculate fees, how revenues generated through these fees will be handled, accounting procedures, and wage scales for part-time instructors.

The National Recreation and Park Association recognizes six types of fees that may be used by a recreation department. These fees are: entrance fees, admission fees, rental fees, user fees, license or permit fees, and special services fees. Since these fees cover different aspects of recreation, they may be used in conjunction with each other at the same location. For example, a park may have an entrance fee to gain entry into the area, a rental fee for paddle boats, and a user fee to use a water slide facility.

Determining fee amounts

Three methods of determining the fee amount are generally used: arbitrary pricing, pricing not associated with cost factors (competitive and variable pricing), and pricing according to cost. Arbitrary pricing merely sets a fee based on the whim of the director. Competitive pricing (charging what others charge) and variable pricing based on what the participant is able to pay are examples of setting fees not associated with cost factors. Although these two methods are used extensively in the field, neither is satisfactory if the department is truly dedicated to increasing revenues through the use of fees.

The third method of pricing is based on the actual costs of offering the program or providing the facility. The cost of providing the program or facility can be broken into fixed costs, direct costs, indirect costs, and capital expenditures. Normally, fixed costs and capital expenditures are not used in computing the fee amount since these two factors would probably increase the fee to unreasonable levels. Direct costs are those expenses which are incurred in conducting the program or operating the facility. If the program had not been offered, no cost would have been incurred. Indirect costs are those expenses which are not directly incurred by the program or facility but may be charged to it—for example, part of the athletic director's salary.

If only direct and indirect costs are to be used in calculating the fee, the total of these costs is divided by the expected number of participants. This yields the program or facility fee. Often a contingency or service fee may be added to this amount. This contingency or service fee is in excess of the actual costs. These "excess" monies may be needed later if the expected number of participants does not materialize or if expenses are higher than expected. Or the money may be used to defray the cost of another program which is not completely self supporting.

If fees are going to be collected by the recreation department, it is imperative that sound accounting procedures be developed so that a strict account for all monies received can be made. This should include a three-copy receipt system, prompt deposit of all funds, and a clear audit trail for each transaction.

An accounting concept that is rapidly gaining acceptance in the field is the use of a special account for departmental revenues. Traditionally all revenues generated by a recreation department have been deposited into the general fund account of the community or county and these revenues are reallocated in the budgeting process the following year. A special account would be an account into which all revenues generated by the recreation department are deposited and from which all expenses incurred by the specific programs are paid. Obviously this type of account would have to be approved by the governing authority of the department. The primary advantages of this type of accounting system are in the accountability of the department (demonstrable efficiency) and in strengthening programming incentives. It should be noted that a special account of this nature is different from an "enterprise fund account," which is used with specific facilities.

Fees for non-residents   When a fee system is set up in a community, questions often arise concerning participation of non-residents. If non-resident participation is great enough to impact the program or increase the expenses of the program, some adjustment in the amount of the fee should be made. Perhaps the easiest and most accurate method of assessing the additional amount of the non-resident fee is through use of the community property tax base. If 25 percent of the general budget of the community comes from property taxes then it is safe to assume that 25 percent of the support of the program or facility comes from this source. Since the non-resident does not pay these property taxes, a non-resident fee can be determined by multiplying the fee amount paid by residents by the percentage of the budget supported by property taxes. This will yield a dollar amount that should be paid by non-residents in addition to the usual program fee.

Fees for facility use   A source of revenue often neglected by a recreation department is a fee for the use of departmental facilities. An additional fee could be collected for exclusive use of the facility, facility use during prime times or where there is a definite difference in the quality of the facilities. For example, an additional fee could be assessed for a group to reserve the use of a picnic shelter or if a softball team wanted to use a field for an exclusive practice. It is also easy to justify a higher fee for newer facilities, and such a differential facility fee system would also aid in redistribution of facility use.

Memberships   Memberships have long been used by private and quasi-public organizations. There are numerous activities and facilities within a recreation department that could utilize a membership fee approach rather than the traditional fee system. Under a membership fee system, facilities such as tennis courts, golf courses, and swimming pools or activities such as youth or adult sports and arts/crafts programs could be paid for on an annual basis for either an individual or for a family. The advantage of a membership to the individual or family would be slightly reduced fees; the advantage to the department would be in receiving funds in advance, which helps in budget planning. Different types of memberships could be made available as well as different modes of payment, such as the use of a bank credit card or bank draft.

Fee waivers   Many departments have developed a policy of fee waiver for individuals who cannot afford to pay for a program or facility. Numerous methods of determining eligibility for fee waiver are used, including tax forms, confirmation by a local welfare agency, or departmental forms. In addition to a complete waiver of fees based on need, many departments use scholarships from businesses or local civic groups to help defray the fee for an individual.

Many departments also allow the individual to "work off" the fee by doing some token job around the department. Before pursuing this approach of "working off" a fee, the department should closely examine all of the legal aspects. Under certain circumstances the department could incur legal responsibilities for the individual who is "working off" a fee.

Public relations   Public acceptance of an increase in an existing fee system or of a newly initiated system is always hard to gauge. Good public relations efforts through the media prior to initiation of the new fees is essential. The most effective methods of winning public acceptance of these new fees will be through generating an understanding of why the fees are necessary and exactly where the money is being spent. For example, an explanation that the entry fee for a softball team is spent on conducting that program, umpire's fees, equipment costs, lighting, and facility maintenance, will usually satisfy any questions. Early promotion of fee increases is also effective: advertising that there will be a fee increase *next year* will circumvent many problems.

Conclusion

Recreation departments will continue to face budgetary problems for the foreseeable future. Restricted or diminished budgets can only be met by either reducing the staff and services offered by the department or by seeking additional sources of revenue. Fees and charges are an additional source of revenue which have traditionally been overlooked or neglected by recreation departments, but the budget crunch will force recreation departments to more fully utilize this revenue source.

How to Establish a Price for Park and Recreation Services

John L. Crompton

The approach to establishing a price discussed in this article consists of three stages. These are illustrated in Figure 1. Stage 1 requires an agency to determine what proportion of the costs incurred in delivering a service should be recovered from direct pricing. Stage 2 recognizes that a service's price has to be perceived as reasonable by potential client groups or they will refuse to pay and/or will vigorously protest through the political process. Using surveys to determine the going rate charged for similar services by other agencies and/or the commercial sector may lead to the cost-based price devised in Stage 1 being adjusted downwards to ensure that it is perceived as "reasonable." In Stage 3 the appropriateness of varying this price for some user groups or in specified contexts is considered.

Stage 1: Determine the proportion of costs which the price should recover

A determination of the proportion of costs which a price is intended to recover is predicated on the assumption that an agency knows the costs of delivering the service. Unfortunately, current accounting systems in many park and recreation agencies are not structured to capture and report cost data for each specific service delivered. They are designed only to provide expenditure information and appropriation control because their purpose has traditionally been to demonstrate compliance as opposed to providing information.

This article first appeared in TRENDS, Vol. 21, No. 4, 1984. TRENDS is cooperatively produced by the National Park Service and the National Recreation and Park Association.

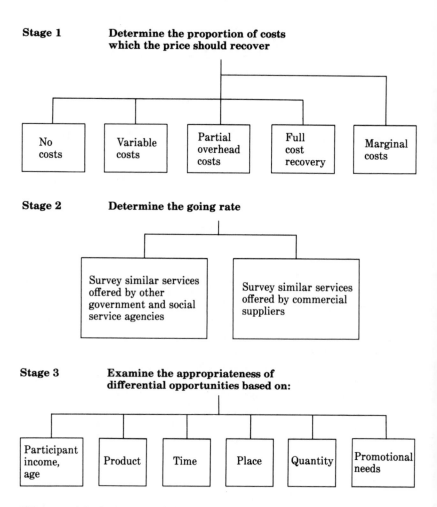

Figure 1. A logical approach to establishing a price.

The critical role of cost accounting   Typically, the cost of providing a service can be viewed as a series of layers.[1] Each layer represents a cost level that must be allocated to the levels beneath and adjacent which benefit from the service. Figure 2 illustrates this typical cost-flow pattern.

The first task in program cost determination is identifying and allocating central service costs to each benefitting department. Typical central service functions are executive administration, purchasing, accounting, personnel, data processing, motor pool, and budget.

After all central service costs have been allocated to the direct service departments, a framework should be developed for allocating the departmental indirect costs to the agency's operating divisions. Departmental indirect costs generally will be a combination of central service costs allocated to the department and the department's administrative support activities costs.

The final task requires that a comprehensive cost be developed for each service which is delivered. This method of cost accounting involves layering costs and then allocating the costs to successively lower echelons of the agency until a true service cost is developed. Cost information permits managers to present the citizenry with a clear statement of the diverse and perhaps substantial financial resources necessary to support each service delivered.

If there is resistance to a formal cost accounting system, then

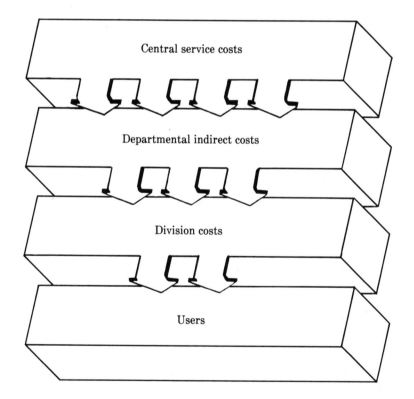

Adapted from Robert D. McRae, "The Cost Burden Study: A Method for Recovering Costs from Non-residents," *Governmental Finance* (March 1982), 10.

Figure 2. A typical cost-flow pattern.

cost finding, which is a less rigorous approach, may be adopted. Cost finding is a less formal method of cost estimation which uses available financial data or finds costs from budget details, the budgetary accounting system, analysis of detailed transactions (such as payroll records, invoices and contracts) and interviews with staff. These data are collected, assembled on worksheets and analyzed to determine individual service delivery costs.[2]

It is rare for an agency's accounting system to provide the complete cost information essential to intelligently determine an appropriate price. In most instances cost finding rather than cost accounting has to be used. This situation exists because in the past, there was no incentive to develop an elaborate cost accounting system since prices were infrequent and nominal, tax-supported budgets were expanding (so no trade-off decisions between services

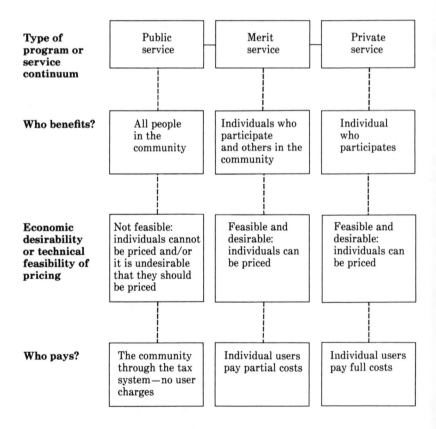

Type of program or service continuum	Public service	Merit service	Private service
Who benefits?	All people in the community	Individuals who participate and others in the community	Individual who participates
Economic desirability or technical feasibility of pricing	Not feasible: individuals cannot be priced and/or it is undesirable that they should be priced	Feasible and desirable: individuals can be priced	Feasible and desirable: individuals can be priced
Who pays?	The community through the tax system—no user charges	Individual users pay partial costs	Individual users pay full costs

Figure 3. Differences between services establishing public, private, and merit characteristics.

were necessary), and the relative cost efficiency of alternative delivery methods such as contracting out was not a concern. Increasingly in the future a cost accounting system is likely to be recognized as an essential management tool. Without such data, opponents of pricing decisions can justifiably argue that they are arbitrary.

Public, merit, and private services   Economists classify services into three categories: public, merit, and private services. Much of the debate about whether or not user prices should be levied, and if so at what level, revolves around the classification of the service as one of these three types. The differences between these categories are summarized in Figure 3.

This classification provides the economic rationale upon which decisions about user pricing should be based. It assumes that the objective is to price each program or service at a level that is fair and equitable to both participants and non-participants. It helps the recreation and park manager determine which services lend themselves to monetary pricing, on what basis, at what level, and with what effects.

If a program exhibits the characteristics of a *private service*, its benefits are received exclusively by participating individuals rather than by the rest of the community. It is usually possible to exclude persons who are not willing to pay for the service. There are essential differences between public and private services, but *exclusion* is the key factor which differentiates them. A fence around a drive-in theater or park may be all that is required to convert a public service into a private service.

The case for financing a service through direct charges to the user is clear-cut when the services provided are perceived as private. When someone receives a direct benefit from government it seems only fair and logical that he or she should pay for it. If no benefits from such a service accrue to other citizens in a community, then it is reasonable to expect the users to pay all of the costs.

At the other end of the continuum (Figure 3), a *public* service, in its pure form, is equally available to all citizens in a community. Often this is because there are no feasible ways to exclude any individuals from enjoying the benefits of the service. Because individuals cannot be excluded, it is not possible to implement a user pricing system unless such a system relies upon voluntary payment. Unfortunately, when payment is voluntary, there are likely to be some individuals who become "free-riders" and take advantage of whatever is available, without paying. To prevent this situation, public types of services are financed by compulsory payment through the taxation system.

Public urban parks are frequently cited as examples of services which exhibit public service characteristics, since they are used by a large proportion of citizens. It may be argued, however, that there is no such thing as a pure public service since some citizens always benefit more than others. Those people living closer to the park, or those who pass it each day on their way to and from work, presumably gain more benefit from it than other citizens. Nevertheless, it is reasonable to assert that an urban park is more appropriately located towards the public-service end of the continuum shown in Figure 3.

Viewing public and private types of services as opposite poles of a continuum is helpful in understanding the essential differences between them, but many recreation and park services lie somewhere between the two poles. Such services are called *merit* services. Merit services have been defined in several ways but they are usually considered to be private services that have some public service characteristics. That is, part of the benefit is received by the individual consumer and part is received by the public in general.

Although it is possible to levy user prices for merit services, it is not reasonable to expect users to cover all costs, because there are spillover benefits which are received by the whole community. Users should be subsidized only to the extent that benefits to the whole community are perceived to occur.

Thus, it is sometimes argued that it may be undesirable to impose "reasonable" user charges even when it is technically possible to do so, if it means that certain people will be excluded. If faced with such a price, these individuals may choose to participate less in certain recreation and park services, which may be considered a socially undesirable outcome. Similarly, it may be argued that certain recreation and park amenities improve the physical quality of the townscape or make it a more desirable place to live. For this reason, subsidizing such amenities may be reasonable since they increase the value of everyone's property.

Locating a service on the public-private continuum   An important point in understanding this public-merit-private classification is that the decisions as to where a service should be located along the continuum shown in Figure 3 are defined through political processes. Hence this position may ebb and flow with changes in the values of a community and it is likely that some services will be classified differently in different communities.

For example, a tennis facility in a high income neighborhood may be perceived as a private service from which only participants benefit. Hence all costs incurred should be covered by user prices. An identical tennis facility located in a low income neighborhood may be perceived as a pure public facility, or at least as a merit facility. In this case the whole community is seen to benefit from the

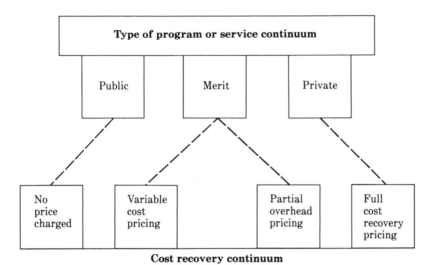

Figure 4. The relationship between type of service and cost recovery strategy.

provision of wholesome activity for its citizens; from improvement of the living environment, which increases the value of all property; or from the psychological satisfaction of knowing that the less wealthy are provided with recreational opportunities which they could not otherwise afford.

Cost-recovery methods   Once an agency has apportioned the relative benefits which each service offers users and the whole community, and thus has classified each of its services as public, merit or private, it is in a position to consider the price which should be charged.

There are three approaches to establishing a price based on recovering some predetermined proportions of costs. These methods relate to the public-private services continuum. The conceptual relationship between positioning on this continuum and these three recovery methods is shown in Figure 4.

Full cost recovery   Full cost recovery is also termed average cost pricing. The price of a service is intended to produce sufficient revenue to cover all the fixed and variable costs associated with the service (these have been defined in the cost accounting system) and enable the break-even point to be reached. Figure 5 shows how to determine a price which is intended to recover full costs.

A price which is intended to recover full costs is determined by using the following formula:
Average cost price = Average fixed cost + Average variable cost

Where:
Average fixed cost = Total fixed costs/Number of users
Average variable cost = Total variable users/Number of users

If: Total fixed costs   = $1000
    Total variable costs   = $ 500
    Projected number of users   =   100

Then: Price = 1000/100 + 500/100

Thus: Price = $15.

Figure 5. Pricing to recover full costs.

Full cost recovery is an appropriate strategy for those services perceived to exhibit the characteristics of private services, which benefit only users and offer no external benefits to the general community. Many recreation and park agencies charge commercial users of their facilities at the full cost recovery level. Examples would include the use of parks by circuses, group picnics, or for filming commercial advertisements; and the use of convention centers or halls for dances, pop concerts, or fundraising dinners.

Efforts to implement a pricing policy which is intended to recover all or some predetermined proportion of costs have to contend with five major problems. First, as discussed earlier, it is difficult to systematically identify, classify, and equitably allocate the costs associated with each service.

Second, the price which is charged will only recover the costs anticipated *if* the projected number of service users is accurate. This may be relatively easy to estimate if historical records are available which show a consistent pattern of participation in a particular program over a period of years. However, if a new service is being introduced there may be considerable error in the participation projection. If the projection is high, and there are fewer users than expected, then the agency will receive much less revenue than it had anticipated when it established the price.

The third problem also relates to accurately projecting the number of service users. (This does not apply when the agency has a monopoly position in the market.) Prices based on recovery of a proportion of costs are determined not by market considerations but by the costs of providing the service. Thus, the prices charged by suppliers of similar services are ignored even though their lower price is likely to adversely impact the number of users of the agency's service. Cost based pricing assumes that client groups are willing and able to pay the proposed price. Particularly in situations where the price is intended to fully recover the costs of delivering a relatively discretionary service, it is likely that client groups may resist it. This may lead to minimum use of a service and consequent erosion of the agency's political support base.

The fourth problem in using cost based pricing is that it may encourage inefficiency. There is a danger that little concern will be given to controlling costs or requiring efficient management since the costs are being directly passed on to users.

The fifth weakness of cost based pricing is that it may lead to an irrational price structure. Consider the implications of the following pricing strategy, which was adopted by an agency which operated a camp facility.

The camp sought to recover all of its costs. Most of the costs were fixed, so the cost of operating the camp was about the same all year round. The prices charged were $80 per three-day weekend in the winter months and $40 per three-day weekend in the summer months. These prices reflected the much higher occupancy rate at the camp in the summer months, which enabled the costs to be spread over more users. However, the price structure had the effect of persuading more people to come in the summer than in the winter. Hence, there were long waiting lists for the summer, but the camp had very low winter occupancy rates.

Full cost recovery pricing is only appropriate for some services. Many services do not exhibit the characteristics of a pure private service because frequently people other than the individuals using the service receive *some* benefits from it. In these merit service situations an agency should seek to recover only partial overhead costs or variable costs.

Partial overhead cost recovery   If the intent is to recover partial overhead costs, then a price is established which meets all direct operation and maintenance costs and some proportion of fixed costs. The remaining proportion of the fixed costs which it is intended to recover represents the tax subsidy given to the particular service. Figure 6 shows how to determine a price which is intended to recover partial overhead costs.

Conceptually, the proportion of fixed costs which should be subsidized is dependent upon the extent to which non-users benefit from a user utilizing a service. As the benefits which accrue to non-users increase, the proportion of fixed costs met by the subsidy should increase (Figure 4).

It is important to note that the anticipated per person subsidy is built into the formula. This is a very different approach to the frequent practice of assigning, say, a 20 percent overhead figure to direct operations and maintenance costs, because this latter approach does not indicate the extent to which individuals are subsidized. If it is decided that a service should be subsidized then the

---

A price which is intended to recover partial costs is determined by the following formula:

Partial overhead recovery price =
Average fixed cost + Average variable - Average subsidy

Where: Average subsidy represents the amount to which each user is subsidized out of tax funds.

If: Average fixed cost   = $8
     Average variable cost   = $4
     Average subsidy   = $3

Then: Partial overhead recovery price = $8 + $4 - $3

Thus: The service would be priced at $9.

Figure 6. Pricing to recover partial overhead costs.

subsidy should be made explicit in the budget and built into the authority's financial control system. This is important because managers responsible for services should set performance targets based on costs, subsidies and targets.

Lack of attention to subsidies expressed on a per unit or per capita basis is likely to lead to substantial inefficiency in the allocation of resources and inequities in service delivery. Users of Service A may be receiving much larger subsidies per capita than users of Service B, even though the price they pay is the same, because the costs of operating the two services are substantially different.

Variable cost recovery   If variable cost recovery pricing is used, the established price is equal to the average variable cost of providing a service. In this context, variable costs are used synonymously with direct operating and maintenance expenses. No attempt is made to contribute toward meeting fixed costs. Figure 7 shows how to determine a price which is intended to recover variable costs.

Because direct operating and maintenance expenses can be easily documented, there is a tendency to base price decisions upon them. This is a popular approach with many agency personnel because

---

A price which is intended to recover total variable costs is determined by the following formula:

Variable cost recovery price = total variable costs/Number of participants

If: Total variable cost   = $500
     Projected number of participants   = 100

Then: Variable cost recovery price   = $ 5.

Figure 7. Pricing to recover variable costs.

when fixed costs are omitted, a relatively low price can be charged and a larger client support constituency is likely to emerge. However, it is also argued that the facilities and amenities offered by recreation and park agencies add to the quality of life or to the "livability" of a community. There are benefits to some non-users from knowing that facilities exist (this "opportunity to acquire" is sometimes called "option demand"), and non-users should therefore pay the indirect fixed costs required to make these amenities and facilities available.

Stage 2: Determine the going rate price

At the end of Stage 1, a provisional price should be determined based upon the proportion of costs which it is expected to recover. However, pricing based on costs is not market oriented because it assumes that service users will pay the suggested price. This may be a false assumption. Cost based pricing also ignores the impact which this price may have on other suppliers of the service. Stage 2 of the process for establishing a price is intended to ensure that the provisional, cost based price is adjusted, if necessary, so it is responsive to the willingness and ability of users to pay and to the impact of the price on other suppliers (Figure 1).

Determining the going rate requires that a survey of prices charged by other suppliers of this service be undertaken. Usually this survey will be confined to other public recreation and park agencies, but in situations where a service is also offered by commercial suppliers they should be included in the price survey. For example, if a department offers campground services it should include private campgrounds in its going rate survey. The agency may then adjust its cost based price in order to ensure that the public campground opportunities do not impede the success of private campgrounds or reduce the range of campground opportunities available. If the public facility charges substantially less than private suppliers it might be detrimental to these suppliers and may lead to congestion of the agency's own facilities.

Adjusting a price so it is consistent with the going rate has two major advantages. First, it may be argued that the going rate price range represents the collective wisdom of professionals and elected officials from other jurisdictions as to what constitutes a reasonable price. For this reason, a price within the range will probably avoid controversy and be regarded by most publics as "fair." For example, if the survey reveals that an agency's prices are lower than those charged by others for a similar service, then it provides strong justification to both user publics and elected representatives for an increase in price.

Some may argue that instead of reflecting the conventional wisdom of the field in price decisions, a survey of prices charged by others serves only to pool the field's collective ignorance! That is, few of the other jurisdictions have any rationale for the price they charge, so using their prices as a guide in a pricing decision only compounds irrationality.

However, a major advantage accruing from comparing existing prices with those charged for similar services elsewhere is that it establishes the *range* of prices which are likely to be acceptable to users of a particular service. It is possible that services may not be exactly the same quality or serve identical types of client groups, but in most cases there are likely to be substantial similarities between services.

Determining the going rate forces an agency to address what potential client groups are willing to pay for a particular service. It is a misconception to believe that costs should necessarily determine price, for often the prices which an agency charges may be used to determine costs. For instance, if a craft program is being priced, an agency might first try to find out what prices it can reasonably expect its potential client groups to pay. When it has this information the agency works backwards from this figure to determine the nature of the materials, equipment and facilities which are suited to such a price.

The going rate price is not "the manager's impression" of what others are charging. It is found by formally surveying what is being charged elsewhere. It may be argued that if the provisional price based on recovery costs in Stage 1 is to be substantially adjusted so it is in accord with the going rate, then Stage 1 may be omitted. This would be a mistake. The going rate often bears little relation to the cost of provision. As a result, if Stage 1 were omitted, sound financial management would not be possible and substantial inequities between services might emerge as some would be more heavily subsidized than others. Without Stage 1 a jurisdiction would not be able to consciously trade off the opportunity cost of one service compared to another, and would not know whether it should price a service at the high or low end of the range of going rate prices.

Stage 3: Examine the appropriateness of differential pricing

At the end of Stage 2, the adjusted price is accepted as the average price which service users should be charged. However, Stage 3 recognizes that there are occasions when offering variations of this price to particular groups may achieve more equitable and efficient service delivery (Figure 1).

Examining the appropriateness of differential opportunities means that an agency considers charging a different price to different groups for the same service, even though there is no directly corresponding difference in the costs of providing the service to each of those groups. Such market oriented price adjustments assume that the market is segmentable and the segments show different price elasticities of demand. A fundamental requirement for an agency to be able to offer the same service at two or more prices is that it must not arouse resentment from a majority of clients, or else antipathy will be created and goodwill lost.

There are six criteria available for dividing a clientele into distinct user groups within which there may be differential pricing opportunities: participant category, product, place, time, quantity of use, and incentives to try. Although each is discussed separately, there are sometimes opportunities to use some of them together.

Price differentiation on the basis of *participant category* is usually related to a perception that some groups may find it difficult to pay a recommended price. Three groups are frequently identified as being less able to pay. They are children, senior citizens, and the economically disadvantaged. Differentials for each of these groups are widely used by recreation and park agencies, although the rationale for offering services at a reduced price to senior citizens has been challenged in recent years because of the elderly's substantially improved economic status.[3]

Differential pricing on the basis of *product* may be used to offer client groups extra levels of service, for example, in park maintenance, or by lighting sports facilities. The agency would provide a basic level of service at a designated price, but those clients who wanted a higher level could receive it by paying a higher price. The prices for these added services would be set to cover the incremental costs of providing them.

Pricing that differentiates on a *place* basis is commonly practiced at spectator events. For example, at a concert, theater or sports event a higher price is charged for front-row than for back-row seats.

The most common use of price differentials based on place relates to higher prices charged to non-residents. Such differentials are relatively easy to impose since non-residents are likely to have relatively little political influence outside their own jurisdiction. The rationale for such pricing is that residents frequently pay at least some of the costs associated with a service through their property taxes, while non-residents make no such payments. This rationale may not be appropriate if services are paid for from other tax sources, for example a sales tax. In this case, people living outside the community may legitimately argue that since they purchase a variety of goods from within the community, they have contributed their fair share of sales tax. Hence, there is no rationale for charging them more than residents for use of these services.

At the municipal level, the authority of agencies to impose differential prices based on residence varies between states. As a result, such agencies must be aware of relevant statutes and court decisions in their particular jurisdictions to determine their authority to impose a different price for non-residents.

If a service is being used to capacity, then a high differential price may be an effective method of discouraging non-resident use. However, if a service has spare capacity, then an agency may want to attract as many outside residents as possible who are willing to pay a price which is higher than the variable cost of servicing them. The revenue accruing from this price will make a contribution to fixed costs and so the service will require less subsidy from taxpayers.

The major problem in establishing differential prices for non-residents is implementation. In those situations in which a client has to show proof of residence each time a service is used, then the irritation of nuisance cost to local residents required to do this may offset any financial gain. This problem does not exist when proof of residence must only be established periodically. Most states, for example, charge substantially higher annual hunting and/or fishing license fees to non-residents than to residents. Proof of residence, in the form of a driver's license or similar document, must only be provided by residents once each year.

In using differential prices on a *time* basis, lower prices are charged for services that are identical except with respect to time of use, in order to encourage fuller and more balanced utilization of capacity. The intent is to encourage use of services at off-peak times and to ration use during peak times.

Quantity discounts are deductions from the regular price that reflect economies of purchasing in large quantities. The most common form of quantity discount used by park and recreation agencies is the season or multi-use pass offered at facilities such as swimming pools, golf courses, and art complexes. Their use has been challenged as being inequitable in some recreation and park situations,[4] but in others their use may be an important part of overall marketing strategy. The basic purposes of a quantity discount are (1) to stimulate additional demand, and (2) to reduce the costs of meeting that level of demand. If these two conditions are not met, then an agency should reconsider its use of quantity discounts.

Price discounts can be used as an *incentive* to persuade people to try a service. New clients may be offered prices lower than those paid by established patrons in the hope of encouraging them to become regular users. It is important that such discounts be selective. Those receiving the discounts should recognize that they are for a limited duration or restricted to a particular set of circumstances, and that after a given time period or change of circumstances the regular price will be charged.

Concluding comments

The systematic approach to deriving a price which has been presented here has to be tempered with a realization that there are two factors which may cause elected officials and potential client groups not always to respond positively to rational pricing decisions. First, a logically derived price may have to be adjusted to accommodate the psychological reactions of targeted client groups. Their reactions to price changes are often irrational, stemming from historical perspectives, analogous experiences, self-interest, or emotion. These dimensions have been addressed by the author elsewhere.[5]

A second qualifying factor is the prevailing political environment which surrounds any pricing decision. Pricing is one of the most technically difficult and politically sensitive areas in which recreation and park managers have to make decisions. Pricing decisions are influenced by ideological, political, economic, and professional arguments. However, the debate which accompanies this diversity of perspectives should be focused upon sound principles.

The main failure of existing user price policies is that they have been designed solely or primarily to raise revenue. The prevailing approach is to raise all prices by some arbitrary percentage amount each year. There is little attempt to discover who is benefitting, who is paying, and the level of benefits and payments involved for each service. Even if incremental price increases are based on some acceptable criterion, they assume that the original price was appropriate. If the initial price was arbitrarily derived, then subsequent incremental increases are also likely to result in an arbitrary price.

The reasoned, rational approach discussed here will not always be immediately convincing to decisionmakers. However, the political and rational approaches to pricing are not mutually exclusive. The introduction of better information is not likely to lead to a diminishing of the elected official's vote—indeed, it should strengthen it. If a rational approach is not presented to elected officials, then it can only encourage continuation of irrational pricing according to whatever personal or arbitrary criteria they care to adopt.

1. Robert D. McRae, "The Cost-Burden Study: A Method for Recovering Costs from Non-residents," *Governmental Finance*, March 1982, p. 9.
2. Ross C. Kory and Philip Rosenberg, "Costing Municipal Services," *Governmental Finance*, March 1982, p. 22.
3. John L. Crompton, "The Equitability of Full-Price Policies for Senior Citizens," *Journal of Park and Recreation Administration*, Vol. 2, No. 1, January 1984.
4. John L. Crompton, "Treating Equals Equally: Some Abuses of a Basic Principle in Pricing Public Recreation and Park Services," *Parks and Recreation*, September 1984.
5. John L. Crompton, "Psychological Dimensions of Pricing Leisure Services," *Recreation Research Review*, October 1982.

Are Your Leisure Services Distributed Equitably?

John L. Crompton

The most critical delivery decisions made by public leisure agencies are distribution decisions. Distribution decisions address the question, "Who gets what, when, where and how?"[1] They determine the "winners and losers" in the community with regard to leisure service provision. Indeed, it has been said that "virtually all of the rawest nerves of urban political life are touched by the distribution of urban service burdens and benefits."[2]

Awareness of the importance of distribution issues is likely to grow in the 1980s since this will probably be an era of retrenchment. When services are static or declining in quantity and quality, citizen interest in the fairness of their distribution is likely to be more prominent than when there are financial resources with which to satisfy new demands without taking resources away from existing target markets.

The term "distribution" implies that a service is allocated on the basis of some principle or standard. The generally accepted standard for allocation of leisure services is equity. Equity is a complex concept with many interpretations. It is difficult to define and each definition is met with some disagreement. Every service distribution pattern reflects a conception of equity. Even though it is frequently not articulated, this question is implied whenever decisions are made concerning services.

This article is reprinted with permission from the *Journal of Physical Education, Recreation & Dance* (April 1982): 67–70. The *Journal* is a publication of the American Alliance for Health, Physical Education, Recreation and Dance, 1900 Association Drive, Reston, VA 22091.

The theme of this article is developed more extensively in John L. Crompton and Charles W. Lamb, Jr., *Marketing Government and Social Services* (New York: John Wiley, 1986).

Equity does not necessarily mean equality. They are related concepts but not identical. Both terms derive from the same Latin word, but in the English language each conveys a different concept. Equality has to do with sameness in quantity and quality, while equity involves fairness and justice. As we shall see later, inequality of resource allocation can be used to promote equity in service distribution. Equity addresses the question, "Is the distribution of leisure services in the jurisdiction fair?" Because subjective and normative judgments are involved, there are no "right" and "wrong" concepts of equity, only different opinions.

Alternative standards of equity

Selection of the appropriate standard of equity to guide the distribution of an agency's services may be made from four alternatives. The characteristics and interrelationships between these four standards are summarized in Figure 1. Each of these standards is discussed in the following paragraphs.

Equal opportunity: the starting point   This is probably the most widely accepted standard of equity. Its wide acceptance most

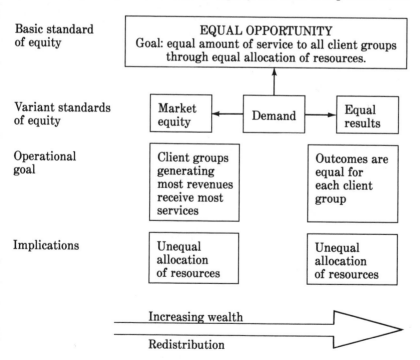

Figure 1. Alternate standards of equity.

likely is a reflection of traditional values which recognize equal protection by the law. *Equal opportunity entails distributing equal amounts of leisure services to all citizens regardless of need or the amount of taxes paid.* An equal opportunity standard would suggest assignment of parks on a per acre, per household, or per person basis. A district with 1,000 residents, for example, might be allocated 10 acres of park land while a district with 3,000 residents might be allocated 30 acres of park land.

Determination of the appropriate standard of equity for a particular service should evolve through consideration of three basic principles:

1. Equal opportunity should be recognized as the norm.
2. Deviations from the norm should have specific justification.
3. There should, in all cases, be a stated minimum level or floor for each service below which quality and quantity should not fall.[3]

This procedure suggests that equal opportunity should be the point of departure from which discussions and decisions about equity should begin. However, it should be accompanied by a range of acceptable deviations which permit other concepts of equity to be applied in appropriate situations (see figure). This deviation range would enable persons with special needs or deficiencies to be allocated more resources in an attempt to achieve *equal results,* or some reconciliation of the amount individuals pay for services with the amount of benefits they receive in a movement toward *market equity.*

However, specific justification should exist for any deviations from the equal opportunity standard, based both on data and on judgment as to the ethics in question. If parks are distributed equally per capita or per household, they probably will not be distributed equally per visit. The overwhelming evidence of empirical studies suggests there may be more visits from people in wealthier neighborhoods. This may provide specific justification for creating more parks in poorer areas and thus deviating from the norm of equal opportunity, toward equal results. Nevertheless, for each area of the city or county a minimum floor level should be stated.

Equal results Equal results entails distribution of services so that outcomes are equal for each individual or area. By this standard an agency should allocate its resources so that all people are in an equal condition after the money is spent. The service is distributed in proportion to the intensity of the need. Equity based on equal results is redistributive in nature (see figure). It implies that an unequal amount of resources, in terms of personnel expenditures, equipment, and facilities, will be devoted to those residents who have greatest need for a service. For example, equal expenditure (opportunity) for maintenance in parks having varying amounts of litter and vandalism is unlikely to result in equally clean parks. Equality of results commonly will require inequality of resources in different areas of a jurisdiction.

Distribution concerned with achieving equal results would allocate bigger and better parks to poorer neighborhoods whose citizens have less private recreational space, and more maintenance personnel to high litter and vandalism parks to achieve equal maintenance levels in all parks.

Perfect equality of results in the distribution of leisure services probably is not a realistic goal. Advocates of the equal results standard of equity often mean "greater equality of results than presently exists." Hence, the operational objective frequently is to increase the compensatory role of public recreation and park services to improve the opportunities of the underprivileged, while recognizing that complete equality may be nonfeasible.

Market equity   Market equity entails distributing services to areas or neighborhoods in proportion to the tax or fee revenues that they produce. In the case of park maintenance, for example, each geographic area in a city would be allocated maintenance personnel in direct proportion to the amount of taxes paid by area businesses and residents. The agency's function, under this equity concept, would be to distribute services but not to engage in any redistribution.

In response to demands to cut local taxes, market equity has been facilitated by charging a direct price for many recreation services rather than fully subsidizing them through the tax system. This standard of equity enhances responsiveness of resource allocation. Citizens do not receive a service they do not want nor are they required to pay for what other citizens consume. They can buy as much or as little of a service as they wish.

Market equity has considerable merit in situations where a distorted income redistribution would otherwise occur, that is, a situation in which poorer citizens subsidize leisure services which are predominantly used by wealthier elements of society. This is a common occurrence, for many recreational and cultural arts services are used by predominantly middle-class citizens, but subsidized out of tax monies collected from all citizens.

Market equity draws from the prevalent distribution model used in the private sector. Full commitment to this equity standard would mean accepting that citizens are not entitled to equal access to outlets, and that citizens' needs are not relevant unless they are backed up by dollar votes in the marketplace. This approach offers the most efficient use of resources but it ignores the social issues associated with equity. Adoption of this standard would mean that many leisure services would be almost entirely removed from poor neighborhoods and relocated exclusively to wealthier neighborhoods. As well as being politically nonfeasible, this probably would violate the public's sense of what is appropriate. Hence, full commitment to market equity is probably inappropriate to society's current standards of what is fair.

Demand: A pragmatic, administrative alternative   Demand entails distributing resources on the basis of consumption and/or vociferous advocacy or complaints. Demand is *not* an equity standard which guides the distribution of services along a predetermined agreed direction. Rather, it is a pragmatic, reactive approach which is administratively convenient, but likely to result in an unpredictable and inconsistent distribution of winners and losers. Demand is shown parenthetically in the figure since in any given situation it may replicate any of the three conceptual alternatives discussed previously or it may inconsistently deviate among them.

On the surface, demand sounds like a reasonable and defensible standard of equity, but it often harbors a hidden distributional bias because if demand itself varies by race or class, the distribution of services will vary by race or class. Because of its administrative convenience and apparent fairness, demand has been widely adopted as the preferred standard of equity. It is particularly characteristic of passive agencies. The limited empirical evidence which is available suggests that demand is more likely to contribute to market equity than to equal results. That is, wealthier citizens tend to be more active and assertive and hence receive more services than poorer citizens when demand is used as the equity standard.

Evaluating equity

Three types of indicators may be used for assessing the equity of existing service and facility distribution patterns.[4] They are indicators based on resources, activities, or results:

1.   *Resources* are inputs to the service distribution system which may include money, personnel, facilities, and equipment.
2.   *Activities* are the way in which the resources are used. For example, the number of recreation programs offered; the frequency with which maintenance crews visit parks; or the number of hours facilities are open.
3.   *Results* are the outputs which measure what happens as a direct consequence of the service delivered. This is the indicator which the average citizen is most likely to use to evaluate services. How clean are the parks? How good are the programs? What benefits do they deliver? How many people use the services?

Different conclusions may emerge from using different methods. For example, recent studies completed by the author in both Austin, Texas, and Metropolitan Dade County, Florida, revealed that low income areas of the jurisdictions have been allocated a disproportionately large amount of *resources* in terms of both capital and operating budgets. In addition, more recreation programs are offered in those areas than elsewhere (an *activities* measure). However, these groups participate much less frequently than do citizens in other areas of the jurisdictions (a *results* measure). Hence, it is important that, as well as determining the concept of equity under which the agency provides services, a decision is made as to which type of measure is most appropriate for evaluating the existing situation.

Four approaches to measuring equity

The major operational difficulty in measuring the equitableness of recreation and park services lies in assessing the benefits offered by very different services. For example, how can the recreation and park resources in Neighborhood A, composed of four small parks, one large swimming pool, three ball parks and a golf course, be compared with those of Neighborhood B, which consist of two large parks, three small swimming pools and one recreation center? These are very different combinations of amenities, and yet they all seek to provide recreational benefits. There are four possible approaches to making such comparisons.

Visual approach   By inventorying and mapping the existing outlets for each service, and by developing transparent overlays for each service, visual identification of relatively deprived and relatively well-endowed areas, in terms of the quantity and quality of services, can be identified. This information also can be computerized, using a code for each street and block. In this way comparisons among services for each block in a jurisdiction would be possible. The main strength of the visual approach is also its major weakness. It is relatively simple to do because the use of subjective, normative judgment avoids the difficulty of trying objectively to weigh the value of a recreation center against the value of a park or a swimming pool.

Standardize provision   Provide each neighborhood the same number of parks, swimming pools, and recreation centers. However, such standardization would probably be inappropriate since citizens in different neighborhoods are likely to have different service priorities.

Activity indicator   Participation or visitation could be used to facilitate equity comparisons. Lower total use of a set of neighborhood facilities (unequal results) may be interpreted to indicate unequal opportunity. However, low use of facilities may occur because there is less interest or demand for the services offered, as well as because opportunities to use the service are not readily available.

Investment inventory   This measures the current appraised value of all facilities and identifies neighborhood inequities through different service areas. Investment in swimming pools, parks, recreation centers, playgrounds, and cultural facilities would be aggregated to identify current investment value of facilities in each neighborhood.

The process is simplified because consistent standardized average investment values for each type of facility have to be used in each neighborhood rather than the real investment values, which will differ between neighborhoods. This is important since investment value in itself serves no service purpose; it is the amount and quality of service opportunity which is relevant. Equity in investment value (resource inputs) may lead to very inequitable opportunity or results if, for example, land is much more expensive in one area of town than another. Hence, some average value is needed.

This investment inventory approach facilitates making budgetary decisions for distributing services among city neighborhoods so that inequities between neighborhoods are reduced. At the same time, it enables the more detailed decisions on which particular types of services should receive priority in each neighborhood to be made flexibly, according to differing neighborhood needs.

In the past, leisure service agencies could often respond to claims of inequitable treatment in service distribution by increasing the total budget and allocating greater resources. Today, the allocation of a greater proportion of the resources to one group will usually lead to a reduced allocation of resources to other groups. In this changed environment, the question of service distribution—"Who gets what"—may need to be rephrased as "Who keeps what and who loses what."[5]

When a service is offered, it nurtures a constituency and establishes a level of expectation and dependence. Reduction of an accustomed service level may generate dissent and invite closer scrutiny of the fairness of the service's distribution, because it exerts a direct and visible adverse impact on the quality of the lives of individuals who compose the constituency. This dissent is likely to be particularly acute in urban areas where heterogeneous groups coexist in close proximity.

Three conceptually different standards of equity have been described, together with the administratively convenient standard of demand. Clearly, they lead to very different patterns of service distribution. Four different approaches to measuring equity have been suggested. The preferred standard of equity will increasingly have to be addressed and deviations from it will have to be demonstrated in an era of retrenchment in order to justify redirection of resources. It seems unlikely that the equity issue can be ignored and permitted to emerge as an unintended consequence of service delivery.

1. Adapted from Lasswell, Harold O. *Politics: Who gets what, how.* New York: McGraw-Hill, 1936.
2. Lineberry, Robert L. *Equity and urban policy.* Beverly Hills, CA: Sage Publications, 1977, p. 13.
3. Lucy, William H., Gilbert, Dennis, and Birkhead, Guthrie S. Equity in local service distribution. In *Public Administration Review* November/December 1977, pp. 687–697.
4. Lucy, William H., and Mladenka, Kenneth R. *Equity and urban service distribution.* Washington, DC: National Technical Information Service, 1977.
5. Masotti, Louis H., and Lineberry, Robert L. *The new urban politics.* Cambridge, MA: Ballinger, 1976, p. 11.

PART 4

Liability and
Risk Management

The Insurance Crisis: A Dilemma for Parks and Recreation

Joseph J. Bannon, Jr., and Lauren B. Bannon

In the past several years, there has been extensive news coverage of what is popularly referred to as the "liability insurance crisis." The volume of information with which the public has been bombarded, however, has not necessarily clarified the situation. Instead, the statistics, accusations, and opinions disseminated by the media have sometimes led to an information overload that makes it difficult to distinguish fact from fiction. This article attempts to sort out the facts and define the nature and magnitude of the liability insurance crisis. The article begins with a discussion of the implications of the crisis for municipal entities, particularly providers of parks and recreation services. The next topic is the causes of the crisis as identified from a variety of perspectives. The final section of the article is devoted to responses to the crisis—public reaction, legislative activity, and recommended actions for municipalities.

Impact of the crisis on municipal entities

Municipalities are scrambling for liability insurance coverage in a shrinking market. When coverage is available, municipal officials and administrators face difficult choices as they try to fit the cost of the insurance into their budgets. A natural response to the crisis has been an increase in taxes and user fees. With insurance premiums exploding upward by as much as 1,000 percent, however, passing the increased cost on to consumers is rarely a viable response.

In some cases in which municipalities have temporarily been without liability insurance coverage, officials and employees have declined to perform their duties, out of fear that they would be held personally liable for municipal activity in the absence of insurance protection.

A more widespread impact of the liability insurance crisis is curtailment or elimination of municipal programs and services. The public looks to the schools, parks, and municipal recreation divisions as the traditional providers of athletic programs and leisure activities, especially for the nation's youth. This traditional role of American municipalities, however, is now being threatened by the inability to insure against the risks inherent in such activities.

In one New York town, officials responded to the liability insurance crisis by ordering removal of all municipal pool diving boards, requiring users of baseball fields to provide their own insurance, cutting a number of athletic programs, and proposing a ban on surfing at municipal beaches. In North Carolina, a county parks and recreation division cancelled its 1986 summer youth camps and backpacking and rafting excursions. Municipalities across the nation have removed playground equipment from parks, padlocked roller skating rinks and other recreational facilities, and generally eliminated recreational programs rather than pay exorbitant premiums or take the chance of paying even larger sums as damages in a lawsuit.

Yet another impact of the insurance crisis is the impairment of existing park and municipal contracts for facilities or services. For example, the Chicago Bears football team leases Soldier Field from the Chicago Park District; part of the lease requires the Park District to provide $100 million general liability insurance and $100 million liquor liability insurance. A few weeks before the beginning of the 1986 football season, the park district had obtained at least $85 million in general liability coverage, but none of the companies bidding for stadium beer concession rights had been able to obtain more than $50 million in liquor coverage. Claiming that the park district has failed to hold up its end of the bargain, the Bears may use the lapse in insurance coverage to attempt to escape from the lease, which otherwise binds them until 1999. Loss of the Bears to a suburban stadium would certainly have a devastating impact on the park district's finances.

Causes of the crisis

The question of what has caused the liability insurance crisis provokes extremely different answers depending on who is asked. Some blame the crisis on the insurance industry, while the insurance industry presents itself as a victim of what it calls the "lawsuit crisis."

Insurance industry viewpoint Members of the insurance industry believe that the problem originates in the public's growing tendency to redress grievances through the courts, the increasing size of judgments, and the escalation in associated legal expenses. According to industry spokespeople, in order to cover the increased volume of claims for payment of these judgments and legal expenses, insurance providers have been forced to raise premiums and reduce the availability of coverage.

In the view of the insurance industry, the sheer volume of lawsuits filed in American courts today is indicative of a crisis. Between 1960 and 1983, the number of civil suits filed in U.S. district courts alone increased 300 percent;[1] the total number of civil suits is increasing annually by 5 to 10 percent.[2] Tort suits increased by 62 percent between 1975 and 1986.[3] Product liability suits rose from 1,600 in 1974 to 13,554 in 1985.[4] Between 1979 and 1985, claims against municipalities increased 141 percent.[5]

Observers have offered a variety of reasons to explain the increase in civil lawsuits. A number of sociologists and economists believe that Americans have become less likely to accept responsibility for their own misfortune and more likely to look for someone else to bear the blame. Others note that increased urbanization may have made it psychologically simpler to sue—because the defendant is often a faceless entity instead of a neighbor. From the insurance industry's perspective, the lure of multimillion dollar judgments has created an additional incentive to resort to the courts.

Not only are there more civil lawsuits filed in our courts today, but the dollar amount of damage awards and settlements has also dramatically increased. The number of judgments over $1 million rose from only 7 in 1970 and 50 in 1976 to 401 in 1984.[6] The widespread publicity accorded multimillion dollar verdicts and settlements has made them seem almost commonplace. For example, in 1985, in a suit arising from a playground accident, the Chicago Park District agreed to a settlement guaranteeing payment of $9.5 million, with the possibility of over $29 million if the injured plaintiff lives to seventy-five years of age.[7]

Jurors' attitudes may have a strong influence on the size of these awards and settlements. A *Wall Street Journal* article included some revealing comments from a member of the jury responsible for the $115 million punitive damages award against the founder of ComputerLand, Inc. The juror said, "At first you think, 'Oh my God, this is a lot of money.' But pretty soon, we just accept that if these corporations treat millions of dollars like nickels and dimes, we have to, too."[8] In a case that involved a $64 million award, jurors indicated that they made the award high to account for lawyers' fees, taxes, and the possible reduction of the amount on appeal.[9] Studies show that juries sympathize with injured plaintiffs and grant higher awards when the defendant is a business than when the defendant is an individual.[10] Insurers argue that it is improper to base liability decisions on how much money or insurance a defendant is perceived to have.

The insurance industry points to judges as well as juries as contributors to the crisis in the courts. In the 15 September 1986 issue of *Business Insurance,* Edward J. Noha, Chairman and Chief Executive Officer of CNA Financial Corporation, noted that judges often reinterpret judicial concepts out of compassion for injured plaintiffs.[11] According to Noha, the result has been an erosion of the concepts of responsibility and accountability on which liability principles are based and a movement toward an entitlement system. Franklin Nutter, president of the Alliance of American Insurers, has said that the U.S. legal system has changed so fundamentally and so quickly that insurers no longer have predictable means of measuring risk. "It's not just that the rules have changed, but the rapidity of those changes," Nutter has commented.[12]

The problem of spiraling awards and settlements is compounded by the fact that lawyers' fees and other litigation expenses account for almost half of these amounts. Twenty-five percent of the $12 billion collected annually in liability insurance premiums is used to pay for legal fees.[13]

As the insurance industry sees it, the combination of more lawsuits, larger awards, and increased litigation costs has played a significant role in bringing about its current financial difficulties. The industry reported a $25 billion loss for 1985.[14] Some insurance companies have been forced to discontinue business; in Illinois, a record fifty insurers closed between 1984 and 1986.[15] Insurers say that 1985 was the worst financial year for the industry since the devastating insurance claims resulting from the San Francisco earthquake of 1906.

The opposing viewpoint: Critics of the insurance industry
Although the insurance industry's views are shared in large part by the medical profession, corporate manufacturers, and defense attorneys, insurers have strong and vocal opposition. Consumer rights organizations, small businesses, and numerous representatives of the legal community—from the U.S. Justice Department to the Association of Trial Lawyers of America—are among the critics.

Ralph Nader characterizes insurers' efforts to reform the legal system rather than the insurance industry as a "fundamental antidemocratic supercentralized power grab." In Nader's view, the attempt by insurers to reverse one hundred years of consumer products safety law is driven by a desire to limit the liability of defendants and to limit defendant's interest in public safety.[16]

Insurance industry critics deny that the sheer volume of litigation and the size of damage awards are causal factors, arguing instead that the insurance industry's own mismanagement has created the current crisis. Some even claim that the insurance industry, having suffered investment losses in recent years, deliberately created the crisis to dupe the public into paying increased premiums.

Critics say that insurers have blown the problem of civil litigation out of proportion. According to the National Center for State Courts, the increased number of lawsuits primarily reflects the increase in population;[17] the number of lawsuits per capita filed in the United States is actually smaller today than in the nineteenth century.[18] Critics argue also that statistics on the increased size of damage awards overstate the situation by failing to account for ultimate reductions or reversals of jury verdicts. Moreover, the statistics are not adjusted for inflation. Critics dismiss the "lawsuit crisis" as a stratagem to justify premium hikes and policy cancellations.

Some observers even question whether the insurance industry is experiencing any serious financial difficulty. Marianna Smith, Executive Director of the Association of Trial Lawyers of America, says that only through "voodoo economics" can insurers claim a $25 billion loss and at the same time admit a $13 billion increase in net worth and a 50 percent rise in industry stock.[19]

Though most observers would agree that the insurance industry has been experiencing a modest decline in profitability, critics of the industry reject an unforeseeable number and size of claims as the cause of the drop in profits—and as justification for increasing premiums and reducing underwriting. According to critics of the insurance industry, mismanagement and unsound underwriting practices from 1979 to 1983 caused today's decreasing profits. The high interest rates that prevailed during those years encouraged prolific underwriting. To obtain more premium dollars for high-yield investment, insurers provided coverage to those who would otherwise have been considered unacceptably high risks.

Studies of the insurance industry reveal that the cyclical nature of the business corresponds to the rise and fall of interest rates. When interest rates dropped, as they did beginning in 1984,[20] it was predictable that insurers would increase premiums and become more conservative in their underwriting practices. No one predicted, however, that instead of increasing premiums modestly, insurers would engage in what Joan Claybrook, President of Public Citizen, has called "highway robbery."[21] In February 1986, *Parks and Recreation* magazine commented that the insurance crisis was the result of some insurers "trying to make up for business investments gone sour" and others "panicking because of some multi-million dollar liability judgments."[22]

An objective analysis of the causes of the liability insurance crisis would probably conclude that both the insurance industry and its critics are correct. As noted by the Illinois Department of Insurance, "at a time when the insurance industry in and of itself was going to have a problem, the civil justice system helped it reach crisis proportions."[23]

Responses to the crisis

Just as the varied explanations for the liability insurance crisis have been widely debated, so have the appropriate responses. This section will examine the three most common responses to the crisis: legislative tort reform, improved risk management, and self-insurance alternatives.

Legislative tort reform   Public responses to the current liability insurance crisis have been strong. A recent Harris poll found that 71 percent of Americans believe that current laws make it too easy for people to sue for damages, and 63 percent believe that cash settlements are excessive.[24] Not surprisingly, 65 percent of those polled favor legislation limiting the amount an individual can recover for an injury. A survey of 3,600 local government officials found that more than 80 percent of the officials believe that reforming current liability laws is a "very important" step in resolving the insurance crisis.[25]

In response to this overwhelming public opinion, forty-one states have enacted laws designed to reform the civil justice system and to make liability insurance coverage more available. Similar legislation at the federal level was debated on Capitol Hill in 1986 and was expected to be reintroduced at a later date. Such legislation, popularly known as tort reform, is the most widely publicized, most extensive, and potentially most dramatic response to the liability insurance crisis. What follows is an overview of the various types of reform and of their effects.

Limiting noneconomic damage awards   Perhaps the most popular reform is legislation limiting the amount of damages that can be recovered for noneconomic injuries—such as damages for emotional distress, embarrassment, pain and suffering, and punitive damages. Researchers have found that noneconomic damages make up approximately 40 to 50 percent of total damage awards.[26] Reformers assert that noneconomic damages often bear little relation to the actual injury suffered and are awarded by juries sympathetic to the injured party or interested in punishing defendants who are perceived as financial "deep pockets." Reformers claim that noneconomic damage awards have turned our system of civil justice into a high-stakes lottery that encourages litigation.

Recently enacted limits on noneconomic damages in general tort cases range from a low of $250,000 in Colorado to a high of $875,000 in New Hampshire. Similar limitations have been imposed in Alaska, Florida, Hawaii, Maryland, and Minnesota. A few states limit such damages even further when a municipality or other governmental entity is sued. For instance, the $875,000 cap in New

Hampshire is reduced to $150,000 per person and $500,000 per accident when a governmental entity is the defendant. Similar legislation has been enacted in Montana, South Carolina, West Virginia, and Wyoming. The federal legislation, which failed to pass the Senate prior to the end of the 1986 term, would limit the recovery of noneconomic damages, other than punitive damages, to $250,000 in certain situations.

Besides limiting the amount of noneconomic damages, several states, including West Virginia and Minnesota, have adopted legislation barring any recovery of punitive damages against public entities. New legislation in states such as Iowa, Minnesota, South Dakota, and Alaska now makes it more difficult to recover punitive damages by requiring the injured party to show by a high standard of proof that the defendant's conduct was flagrant, malicious, or in conscious disregard of the safety of others. Finally, three states— Florida, Oklahoma, and Colorado—have enacted reforms that tie the amount of punitive damages to some multiple of the economic damage award. The Colorado and Florida reforms further provide that some portion of the punitive damages awarded to a plaintiff are to be paid to the states' general revenue funds.

Eliminating joint liability   Eliminating the legal doctrine of joint liability has been as popular a reform as limiting noneconomic damages. Under the doctrine of joint liability—also known as the "deep pocket" doctrine—all defendants in a single lawsuit are jointly responsible for paying the entire damage award, regardless of their relative degree of fault. The result is often that the wealthier defendants—usually corporations or municipalities—have to pay the shares of poorer defendants, even if the poorer defendants were primarily at fault.

In a recent Florida case, a Ft. Lauderdale woman was awarded $75,000 for injuries suffered when her fiancé crashed his miniature car into hers on a Disney World ride. The jury found the woman 14 percent liable for her own injuries, her fiancé 85 percent liable, and Disney World only 1 percent liable. However, because the fiancé was unable to pay his $64,500 share of the liability, Disney World was ordered to pay his share of the judgment; Disney World's own share would have been only $750.[27]

Florida is among the states that have recently enacted reforms modifying the doctrine of joint liability. Florida law now provides that in cases involving damage awards of more than $25,000, joint liability applies only to economic damages and only if the fault of the defendant is greater than that of the injured plaintiff. A new Illinois law exempts defendants from the doctrine of joint liability if they are less than 25 percent responsible for the damages, although all defendants remain jointly liable in medical malpractice and environmental suits. Proposed federal legislation would eliminate the doctrine of joint liability for noneconomic damages in product liability suits.

Other reforms modifying or abolishing joint liability have been adopted in Alaska, California, Colorado, Connecticut, Hawaii, Michigan, New York, Utah, Washington, and Wyoming. The Michigan law is particularly interesting because it focuses on public entities: if a defendant fails to pay its share of a damage award, the public entity's share of that uncollectible amount is limited to its percentage of fault in the matter.

Strengthening governmental immunity statutes   Although the liability insurance crisis became the focus of attention in the mid-1980s, states had begun expanding their immunity statutes several years earlier. Colorado passed a 1979 law providing immunity to ski-area operators for certain accidents on the ski slopes. Other states have enacted immunity statutes protecting public and private landowners from liability for accidents on their property involving snowmobiles and off-highway vehicles. California adopted a 1984 statute protecting park and recreation agencies from liability for "hazardous recreation activities."

As a result of the recent tort reform movement, several states have strengthened and expanded their immunity statutes even further. Some have enacted statutes lowering the standard of care that a public entity owes to injured parties. A Tennessee law renders a municipality immune from liability unless it can be proved that the municipality acted willfully, wantonly, or with gross negligence. In Iowa, an injured plaintiff in certain circumstances must now show that the municipality acted with actual malice. In these two states, mere negligence may no longer be sufficient to subject municipalities to liability.

Other states have enacted "recreational use" statutes limiting the liability of private landowners and governmental entities for injuries occurring on outdoor lands. These statutes are designed to recognize the natural dangers associated with certain outdoor activities such as snowmobiling and motorcycle riding. Minnesota and Louisiana have adopted such statutes, and legislation in Illinois extends the recreational use immunity to certain indoor activities. Illinois has further strengthened its immunity statute by specifying that the purchase of liability insurance does not deprive a municipality of its right to immunity under the statute.

Limiting the lawyers   Reform efforts have invariably included criticism of the legal profession. A Harris poll found that 80 percent of Americans believe that "lawyers looking for big contingency fees" is one of the primary reasons for the increased number of lawsuits filed today.[28] The insurance industry and reformers alike claim that plaintiffs' lawyers, who generally receive one-third of an award as their fee, push for higher and higher jury verdicts and encourage needless litigation in hopes of striking it rich in one big case. Reformers also assert that defendants often have to pay settlements in otherwise frivolous cases simply to avoid the risk of an emotional jury verdict.

The most popular response to these concerns has been to impose penalties on lawyers and parties that file frivolous lawsuits and engage in needless delay tactics. Sixteen states have passed legislation requiring a losing plaintiff to pay the defendant's legal expenses if the court determines that the lawsuit was frivolous. In Iowa, if the court determines that a plaintiff has filed three frivolous suits within the last five years, the court can require that plaintiff to post bond covering the defendant's anticipated legal expenses.

Several states have also placed limits on the fees that plaintiffs' lawyers can receive for a single case. Connecticut, for example, has established a sliding scale for contingent fees under which the lawyer's fee cannot exceed 33.3 percent of the first $300,000 of an award; 25 percent of the next $300,000; 20 percent of the next $300,000; 15 percent of the next $300,000; and 10 percent of any amount over $1.2 million. Hawaii and Washington have passed laws giving courts the authority to review the reasonableness of an attorney's fees.

The collateral source rule   In many states, the defendant is not allowed to introduce evidence to the jury showing that the injured plaintiff has insurance coverage or other potential sources of compensation for the injury. Reformers claim that failure to advise a jury of a plaintiff's collateral sources of compensation permits the plaintiff to receive double compensation. In addition, a jury may be motivated to rule in favor of a plaintiff if it appears that the plaintiff will otherwise be left with nothing.

Several states have recently abolished or modified the collateral source rule. These states now permit the defendant to inform the jury of the plaintiff's collateral sources of recovery or require the court to reduce the award by the amount of any collateral payments. The Colorado law, however, provides that awards will not be reduced by the amount of collateral payments if those payments resulted from an insurance policy paid for by the plaintiff. In Alaska, the court can reduce an award by the amount of collateral payments, including insurance coverage, but must give the plaintiff credit for any insurance premiums paid.

The impact of reform   Now that reforms are in place, will insurance rates drop and coverage become more available? The insurance in-

dustry is offering no guarantees. The director of the Washington
Insurance Council cautioned that "there are so many variables on
premiums that it's difficult to tell if premiums will go down."[29] In
California, which passed a public referendum abolishing joint liability, a survey of eighteen insurers by the state's insurance com-
missioner found that only two insurers were willing to begin offering municipal liability coverage without qualification. Five insurers
responded that they were considering reentering the market, and
eleven said that they would reenter the market, but with limitations.[30]

Representatives of the insurance industry have noted that
many of the new tort reforms are being attacked as unconstitu-
tional by plaintiffs' attorneys; until these attacks are resolved by
the courts, it is not clear whether reform has been achieved. The
Association of American Trial Lawyers has established a Constitu-
tional Challenge Committee to coordinate efforts among plaintiffs'
attorneys in various states. The Academy of Florida Trial Lawyers
is already involved in litigation to overturn Florida's recent reforms.

Even assuming that the tort reforms withstand these legal
challenges, the insurance industry contends that many reforms are
inadequate. For instance, the insurance industry and a number of
business leaders perceived the Illinois laws as so weak that they
urged the governor to veto the legislation. The president of the Illinois Manufacturers' Association complained that "poor legislation
such as this is worse than nothing."[31] Business leaders in Minnesota
(likewise unsuccessfully) lobbied the governor to veto that state's
reform legislation. Even in states where the insurance industry and
business leaders have supported the tort legislation, they stress that
further reforms are needed.

Several states have attempted to ensure that the legislative reforms will ease the current crisis by ordering concessions from the
insurance industry in exchange for the reforms. Florida legislation
requires insurers to roll back 1987 premiums to 1984 rates. In Hawaii, insurers are required to reduce premiums by 10 percent in
1986, 12 percent in 1987, and 15 percent in 1988 on all commercial
insurance policies except medical malpractice and commercial auto.
The West Virginia legislature originally considered reforms that (1)
would have required malpractice insurers to give "due consideration" to a policyholder's past claims experience and (2) would have
mandated that rates "shall not be excessive, inadequate, or unfairly
discriminatory." However, these provisions were withdrawn from
the proposed legislation amid cries from the insurance industry
that the proposals usurped their authority to make fundamental
underwriting decisions.

On balance, it does not appear that the impact of the current reforms will be as dramatic as originally hoped. Most insurers appear to be taking a cautious, wait-and-see attitude, although shortly after that state had enacted reforms, one insurer in Washington announced that it would begin providing coverage for risks it had previously deemed uninsurable, including school districts and municipalities with populations of less than 100,000. Ultimately, the most potent weapon against the crisis may be public pressure on the insurance industry, requiring it to support its cries for tort reform by reducing premiums and increasing availability of coverage.

Improving risk management   The twin goals of risk management should be to make the municipal and park district operations more attractive to outside insurance companies and at the same time reduce exposure to liability and financial loss. A well-designed risk management program both identifies and minimizes risks.

To identify existing and potential problems, criteria must be set and data collected. Objective criteria and minimum standards must be established to define problem areas. Systematic recording of loss data allows the cause and scope of any problem to be assessed and analyzed; it also may help demonstrate to insurers that an organization is a sound risk. Once a problem is defined and analyzed, corrective action should be taken to eliminate or minimize the risks involved. Continued monitoring of the situation is necessary to ensure that corrective action is effective. As a risk management program becomes increasingly sophisticated, the focus shifts from reacting to deficiencies to evaluating operations from the ground up.

Structuring a risk management program   The best structure for risk management assigns a central body authority to monitor the overall program. Central authority allows for a more comprehensive view of problems and a more balanced approach to solutions; central authority also helps to build accountability into the system. Finally, naming a central authority demonstrates an organization's commitment to risk management.

A central committee with members from all areas of operations is the best means of drawing upon all resources and bringing together key personnel and constituencies. To ensure governing board or council involvement, it is useful to have a director or council member on the committee. An attorney with expertise in recreation liability also should be a committee member. An attorney will be helpful in identifying legal issues, and if a lawsuit is actually filed can serve as a liaison in handling claims. The central committee should oversee the risk management function throughout the organization, while each department or operating group is responsible for recommending and implementing corrective action in its own sphere.

Prevention and containment   Educating those who use the park
services and facilities is one means of reducing injuries and mini-
mizing consequent liability. Betty van der Smissen notes in "Trends
in Personal Injury Suits" that participants should

1.   Receive complete information about the proper manner in
     which to engage in activities
2.   Be instructed on how to participate safely and in accordance
     with their abilities
3.   Be informed of the risks they assume by participating.

The participant's "assumption of the risk" can be an effective defense against claims of liability for personal injuries.[32]
     Educating the providers and administrators is equally impor-
tant. An operations manual covering topics such as proper use of
equipment, safety instructions to be communicated to program participants, and transportation rules should be kept current and used
by employees. Use of an operations manual will help to eliminate
inappropriate or negligent actions by staff and to document the
organization's policies in the event they are called into question. A
continuing education program will keep personnel up to date about
judicial and legislative developments in the area of tort liability. A
central risk management committee can play an important role in
continuing education by disseminating information throughout the
organization. The more informed staff members are about risk
management, the better equipped they will be to anticipate problems and guard against liability.
     Not only will knowledgeable employees help to avoid accidents,
but if an accident results in a lawsuit, the employee's testimony will
also be of value. In a suit against Walt Disney Productions, a eu-
calyptus tree branch fell and caused a car ride to crash. Disney's
tree expert kept a record on each tree in the amusement park, and
when this conscientious and knowledgeable employee could not explain why the branch had fallen, the jury decided that it was an act
of God and that Disney was not responsible.[33]
     Another protective step available to park and recreation agen-
cies is to ask each adult participant to sign a waiver releasing the
service provider from liability; a parent or adult guardian can sign a
waiver on behalf of any minor participant. A waiver form that is
written clearly and voluntarily signed by an adult may prove a valid
defense to liability. The waiver should include a description of the
activity, associated risks and potential injuries, a statement of
physical conditioning and skills necessary for participation, and an
agreement by the participant to follow instructions and obey the
supervisor.
     If an accident does occur, staff must file a complete report. The
report not only documents the immediate problem but also helps to

prevent similar accidents in the future. Staff should be trained to include only objective statements in accident reports. Subjective comments, such as "It could have been a lot worse" or "We knew this might happen" can create serious problems if litigation arises later.

In a risk management program, spectator safety is as important as that of participants. Proper maintenance of facilities, effective crowd control measures, and available medical assistance are prudent steps to reduce the chances of liability.

Public park and recreation agencies should take a cue from the success of Walt Disney Productions in the private-sector leisure business. Although there are more than thirty million visitors to its amusement parks in California and Florida each year, surprisingly few lawsuits result—a fact that can be attributed, at least in part, to quick soothing by Disney staff if an accident occurs.[34] Disney counsel Mike McCray sums it up: "If people get wet, we've got clothes dryers, and we dry them off. Before they know it, they're back out there having fun."[35] It is not always that easy to soothe someone, but the point is to give a caring impression by immediately attending to the needs of anyone injured while using park services or facilities. To this end, all field employees—especially instructors and coaches—should be trained in first aid techniques, and the training program should be documented.

Disney emphasizes employee preparedness for prompt action in the event of an accident. Employees quickly call in supervisors and security personnel to interview witnesses as well as the injured party. The staff is ready to record on-the-scene admissions of responsibility that injured parties sometimes make.

A risk management program should be a high priority for every public recreation agency. This section has offered a program structure and some basic implementation approaches, but each agency must tailor its risk management program to its own situation. Creativity should be encouraged in determining preventive and corrective actions.

Self-insured alternatives   As traditional liability insurance coverage has become scarce, many public entities have turned to a variety of insurance alternatives. Self-insured pools, the most popular alternative, are created by municipalities and other public entities banding together to self-fund their insurance coverage. Experts estimate that the number of public entities participating in self-funded pools increased to approximately forty thousand in 1986 and that there are now more than two hundred such pools operating throughout the nation.[36] Recent federal legislation removing a number of state barriers to the formation of self-insured pools should encourage this growth even further.

Self-insured pools are most often funded through annual contributions by pool participants. These contributions are usually based on a variety of factors, including the size of the public entity and its prior loss experience. Participants in the recently established Authority for California City Excess Liability Pool must pay annual contributions of 1.2 percent of each municipality's payroll. The intergovernmental pool created by the North Carolina Association of County Commissioners plans to assess its members approximately $.55 per county resident for each of the next three years to capitalize its pool. Several organizations and entities, including Prescott, Arizona, and the Montana Municipal Insurance Authority, have used public bonds to finance their insurance pools. In addition, pool participants can often be assessed some portion of their annual contribution, usually up to 25 percent, to pay claims incurred by the pool in any one year. The insurance coverage provided by these pools varies widely, but in some states meshes with the statutory limits placed on municipal liability.

Congressional approval of the Risk Retention Act of 1986 has opened the door for the creation of larger, nationwide, municipal liability pools. Prior to this legislation, a risk retention group had to obtain rate and policy form approval from every state in which it planned to do business. Under the new legislation, a risk retention group chartered in one state is free to operate nationwide without obtaining prior approval from each state. Municipal and park associations may now develop self-funded liability insurance pools that can be operated on a national scale.

Conclusion

The current insurance liability crisis threatens to destroy the ability of municipalities and park districts to provide basic recreational services to the public. While the causes and potential solutions to the liability insurance crisis continue to be debated, there are indications that the worst may be over. Legislative reforms, while not the panacea originally hoped for, have brought some insurers back into the market and additional reforms may spur other insurers to do the same. In the meantime, efforts by municipalities and park districts to strengthen their internal risk management programs and to explore self-insurance alternatives will help municipalities and park districts contend with the current crisis and better prepare them for any future liability insurance crisis.

1. "Lawyers Not All to Blame for Court Woes: Judge," *Business Insurance*, 3 February 1986, 29.
2. President's Commission on Outdoor Recreation, *Tort Liability in Recreation: A Preliminary Report*, unpublished, n.d.
3. "Courting Disaster: Costs of Lawsuits Keep Growing, and Many Firms Find Insurance Now Is Unattainable," *Wall Street Journal*, 16 May 1986.
4. President's Commission, *Tort Liability*.

5. Linda Collins, "Tort System Twisting Law, CNA Chief Says," *Business Insurance*, 15 September 1986, 18.
6. President's Commission, *Tort Liability*, Insurance Information Institute, *The Lawsuit Crisis*, pamphlet published in April 1986.
7. *Nelson vs. Chicago Park District*, case no. 79L019301, Circuit Court of Cook County, Illinois.
8. Monica Langley, "In Awarding Damages, Panels Have Reasons for Thinking Very Big," *Wall Street Journal*, 29 May 1986, 1.
9. Ibid., 20.
10. Collins, "Tort System Twisting Law," 19.
11. Ibid., 18.
12. Jerry Geisel, "RIMS 1986, U.S. Civil Justice System 'Pretty Terrific,' ATLA Chief Says," *Business Insurance*, 28 April 1986, 4.
13. Royal Oakes, "Don't Make Insurance a Scapegoat," *USA Today*, 14 April 1986, 10A.
14. Marianna Smith, "Don't Put Limits on Right to Justice," *USA Today*, 14 April 1986, 10A.
15. Daryl Strickland, "Lobbyist Sees Insurer 'Blackmail,'" *Chicago Tribune* business section, 7 April 1986, 1.
16. Alberta I. Cook and Michele Galen, "Inside the ATLA Meeting," *National Law Journal*, 28 July 1986, 3.
17. Stephen Tarnoff, "9% Increase in Tort Litigation Not Enough to Be Explosion," *Business Insurance*, 5 May 1986, 1.
18. Joan Claybrook, "Focus Reform Efforts on Insurance Industry," *USA Today*, 14 April 1986, 10A.
19. Smith, "Don't Put Limits on Right to Justice," 10A.
20. Strickland, "Insurer 'Blackmail,'" 1.
21. Claybrook, "Focus Reform Efforts on Insurance Industry," 10A.
22. "The Liability Crisis," *Parks and Recreation*, February 1986, 32.
23. "Insurance Industry, Courts, Share Blame for Crisis: Report," *Chicago Daily Law Bulletin*, 1.
24. Louis Harris, "Those Rising Liability Suits," *Las Vegas Sun*, 12 June 1986.
25. Stephen Tarnoff, "Governments See the Need for Tort Reform," *Business Insurance*, 20 October 1986, 88.
26. Stephen Tarnoff, "Tort Law Must Change to End Insurance Crisis: Researcher," *Business Insurance*, 20 October 1986.
27. "Disney, 1% at Fault, Must Pay 86%," *Chicago Daily Law Bulletin*, 10 April 1986.
28. Smith, "Don't Put Limits on Right to Justice," 10A.
29. Peter Waldman and Eileen White, "Battle Rages over Damages, Insurance Rates," *Wall Street Journal*, 15 April 1986, 6.
30. "Prop 51 Isn't Helping Municipalities: Survey," *Business Insurance*, 25 August 1986, 29.
31. Carol Cain, "Illinois Business Leaders Urge Governor to Veto Tort Reform Bill," *Business Insurance*, 7 July 1986, 2.
32. Betty van der Smissen, "Trends in Personal Injury Suits," *Parks and Recreation*, May 1985, 57–58.
33. "No Mickey Mousing Around," *Time*, 11 March 1985, 54.
34. Ibid.
35. Ibid.
36. Meg Fletcher, "Public Entities Seek Insurance Alternatives," *Business Insurance*, 15 September 1986.

Safety Is No Accident

Monty L. Christiansen

A seven-year-old fell five feet from the top of an elevated slide in a city park.

A young person, sitting on a bench above an eight foot backcourt wall, was hit in the eye with a tennis ball.

A 35-year-old ran into a fence post while playing in an adult softball game.

An 18-year-old fell from a cliff after stepping off a park trail.

These accidents have one thing in common: In each case, the managing leisure service agency was sued for damages and found liable for injuries due to negligence. The sad fact is that these accidents and expensive litigation could have been prevented. Although insurance covered most of the tangible costs, the intangible costs of damaged professional reputations and bad publicity are incalculable.

Courts have traditionally recognized four basic defenses to liability suits involving accidents in park and recreation areas:

1. *Immunity from suit.* Sovereign immunity, formerly a bastion against litigation, has deteriorated recently, and most leisure service agencies may no longer claim it as a legal defense.
2. *Assumption of risk.* Sports participants and spectators have sometimes been found personally liable for injuries incurred as a result of sports accidents. Requiring people to sign general waiver forms to enroll in recreation programs, however, does not protect agencies from negligence suits.
3. *Contributory negligence.* If the injured party was careless or

Reprinted from the May 1985 issue of *Parks & Recreation* by special permission of the National Recreation and Park Association.

> **Risk:** The possibility of incurring harm due to an accident.
>
> **Risk management:** The practice of controlling the possibility and severity of foreseeable accidents; administering due care.
>
> **Negligence:** Ignoring a foreseeable harm and failing to take adequate precautions against it.
>
> **Negligence of commission:** Committing an unlawful act.
>
> **Negligence of omission:** Failing to carry out a legal duty.

was acting under the influence of alcohol or drugs, the defense of contributory negligence may be available. This approach may offer an after-the-fact excuse, but it is not a preventive safety technique. Many states have replaced the concept of contributory negligence with one of comparative negligence, in which the court apportions the blame between the parties.

4. *Due care.* Exercising due care is the most effective preventive technique and the strongest defense against charges of negligence. By adopting this approach *before* any incidents occur, park and recreation agencies can prevent many accidents and can prove that those that do occur are not the result of agency negligence.

   The phrase "due care" implies a professional standard of care. Maintaining due care for ensuring the safety of visitors, which is sometimes referred to as park risk management, involves applying normal caution, procedures reasonable under the circumstances, guidelines, customs, standards, and state-of-the-art safety practices.

   This standard of care cannot be defined in an itemized list of steps to follow in planning, developing, and operating a park. If an accident leads to a liability suit, however, there are several management practices that courts typically examine to determine whether proper consideration was given to the safety of visitors.

   There are four recommended risk management practices related to planning and developing parks and recreation areas.

1. Abating inherent hazards   An inherent hazard is a natural feature of the environment that is potentially dangerous. Examples include rapids or deep pools of water, rock slide areas, dead trees that remain standing with overhanging limbs or weakened trunks that might fall on people, poisonous snakes or other dangerous wildlife, open caves, crevices, steep slopes, and cliffs.

   Two considerations are important. The first is the probability, or risk, that an accident might occur: A cliff in an undeveloped portion of a park is not as apt to cause an accident as a cliff with a popular picnic area located just behind its crest. The second consideration is the potential severity of the injury most likely to result from an accident. For example, a person struck by a falling six-foot sapling is not likely to suffer as much injury as a person struck by a 50-foot tree with heavy overhanging limbs.

Three options are available for abating inherent hazards.

The first and most effective option is to remove the hazard. In some instances this is relatively easy: cutting down dangerous dead trees in active areas. But many hazards are impossible or impractical to remove. In fact, many inherent hazards are what attracts people to the park—a scenic overlook atop a cliff, a waterfall, or a deep cold-water lake.

The second option is to reduce either the foreseeable risk or the potential severity of the accident. This can be accomplished a number of ways, including limiting public access to the hazardous area; erecting safety barriers, guard railings, and fences; routing trails away from the hazardous area except at carefully developed safe locations; or providing lifeguards and guides trained to control public activities and immediately respond to emergencies.

The third option is to provide clear and adequate warning to park visitors and permit them to assume the risk based upon their own judgments of their abilities and the hazard. This option is commonly done by public announcements and feature stories in the news media; by warning signs at key points in the park (such as the entrance, visitors' center, registration booth, restrooms, lodges and cabins, as well as adjacent to the hazard); and by including warnings on park literature (such as brochures, maps, guidebooks, and reservation forms).

To be effective, a warning should not only identify the danger, but should also specify the recommended safe action in an easily understood manner. If the hazard has a high risk to children, a written sign may be an adequate warning.

2. Conforming with standards set by sport, league, or competition-sanctioning organizations Those who plan or develop parks or recreation areas use officially designated dimensions and designs for sportfields, courts, and pools, so that competitive results at these sports facilities will be acceptable to sanctioning organizations such as the Amateur Softball Association of America, the United States Tennis Association, and the Amateur Swimming and Diving Federation.

Another important reason to conform with standards is safety. For example, a serious injury resulted when a man playing in an adult softball league ran into a "safety screen" in front of the players' bench only eight feet from the baseline. ASA standards specify a 25-foot minimum obstacle-free clearance from the foul lines. Official layouts and development criteria for each sport facility should be carefully followed.

3. Complying with public safety codes and regulations Two types of health and safety regulations must be considered. Of primary importance to park and recreation agencies are specific regulations for certain recreation facilities, such as public swimming pools and beaches.

Park agencies may maintain safety criteria more stringent than state minimum standards that are more than ten years old. Such standards and guidelines frequently need updating.

Today, park managers must reject the notion that there are absolute, non-revocable safety standards that remain unchanged over time. Like all other elements affecting recreation, park risk management is based upon contemporary conditions, not those of years past.

Changes in participants, recreation, the level and extent of participation, recreational equipment, facilities, and expectations have affected the basis for risk management. Safety standards must stay current with these changes.

For example, some courts have ruled that safe swimming pool depths are affected by improvements in diving boards and have accepted either the FINA or the National Federation recommendations over less stringent, outdated state regulations. (This does not mean that facilities built in compliance with safety criteria of an earlier time must be considered obsolete and unsafe when new criteria are recognized. But park managers must be reasonable and prudent in light of new knowledge, and cannot ignore the changes.)

Although they are not regulations, the *General Guidelines for New and Existing Playgrounds* (U.S. Consumer Product Safety Commission) have been cited in liability suits against park agencies. Municipal or state regulations spell out health and safety standards for food preparation and eating facilities, vending machines, drinking fountains, sanitary facilities, solid waste, and fire control.

4. Providing facilities for emergencies Park and recreation areas should have emergency facilities designated for circulation, communication, first aid and emergency dispatch, and firefighting.

Emergency circulation routes serve two separate needs. Emergency access routes provide the quickest means of reaching activity centers and designated points in the park for emergency vehicles, such as ambulances, fire trucks, and police vehicles. Emergency evacuation routes to safety for park visitors should be separate from access routes to avoid traffic interference and congestion. Interior evacuation routes leading to emergency exists should be marked on simple schematic floorplans displayed in recreation buildings.

Emergency communications should be readily available at each major facility. This is most commonly a public telephone with a local phone number for reporting emergencies prominently posted nearby. In a large park, the local emergency phone number should be that of a park control center staffed by personnel who are familiar with the park and who can quickly contact the appropriate emergency support service. If the park provides overnight facilities, such as a campground, lodge, or cabins, the emergency phone number should be that of a 24-hour station. It is not sufficient to rely on the telephone company's traditional "Dial 0 for Operator for Emergencies." The operator probably is unfamiliar with locations in the park and might not summon locally available assistance. This would delay response time.

Each park should have properly equipped first aid centers staffed by qualified personnel. If a park is located far away from an ambulance service, an emergency dispatch vehicle that meets the standards for the local jurisdiction should be available in the park.

Parks with buildings or other vulnerable facilities should have adequate fire detection and alert systems as well as interim and primary provisions for fighting fires.

Emergency provisions, including evacuation routes, emergency telephones, first aid centers, and fire extinguishers, must be clearly marked if the public must use them. In addition, the locations of emergency telephones and first aid stations should be prominently posted in every public building as well as shown on park maps distributed to visitors.

There are two recommended risk management practices related to personnel training and responsibilities.

1. Designating a park safety officer Everyone's general responsibility is no one's specific responsibility. Therefore it is important to designate a safety officer. In most departments, this will be a collateral duty. The safety officer must develop a safety plan for the park, including provisions for visitors and employees, and must have the authority to make inspections and require that measures be taken to abate hazards and prevent accidents. The safety officer must receive the training and current information to make appropriate safety decisions.

2. Providing safety training for staff At least once a year, the park safety officer should conduct staff safety training programs, including reviewing current safety standards, investigating accidents, and staging drills of simulated emergencies that might occur in the park.

Five administrative procedures are recommended park risk management practices.

1. Following a written safety policy A written policy on visitor safety should guide risk management decisions about identifying and abating hazards, prohibiting unsafe actions, setting standards for maintenance and upkeep, and providing for emergency services. This policy should be strictly enforced.

2. Conducting routine inspections and hazard abatement An outdoor inspection is advisable two or three times annually—pre-season, mid-season, post-season—in areas that have imposed hazards, such as structures, pavement, swimming pools, buildings, and play apparatuses. The inspection should be documented on a form based on applicable local codes, regulations, and development standards.

In natural public use areas such as rustic campgrounds or hiking trails, which generally have more inherent hazards than imposed hazards, a recorded inspection should be made at least annually. All potential hazards should be identified, with notations of their exact locations, the levels of risk to the public, and the degree of severity for the most likely accidental injuries.

Following the hazard inventory and assessment, park officials should initiate a pre-established hazard abatement program, prescribing corrective measures, priorities, and a schedule. The priority of maintenance assignments should reflect the assessments of risk and severity of foreseeable injury.

Copies of these routine hazard inspections and follow-up abatement practices can be offered as evidence of due care in suits alleging negligence due to improper management and poor maintenance.

3. Helping park employees and visitors report hazards Hazards may become dangerous quickly even when a routine safety inspection has just occurred. Therefore, it is wise to have a clear, convenient, and meaningful method for employees and visitors to report hazards immediately.

Basic information to ask for can be as simple as "What?, Where?, When?, and Who?". What?—the general type of hazard; Where?—its location; When?—the time and date it was noticed; Who?—the name of the person reporting the information. Posters and notices in visitor centers, restrooms, campgrounds, rental cabins, and lodges can instruct park visitors about how to report hazards. This also illustrates the concern the park department has for visitor safety.

The quickest way to report a hazard may be different for each area of the park. Campers may report to campground hosts, managers, or the camp store operator; swimmers may report to lifeguards or pool managers; cabin renters may contact the park office. As standard procedure, the visitor should be asked to wait and take a park employee to the hazard. Response to these reports should be prompt. The first action may be to prevent access to the hazardous area and to post temporary warnings to prevent an accident until permanent corrective measures can be taken. Employees should follow a similar procedure to report a hazard.

4. Using written emergency procedures Written emergency procedures should be prepared and distributed to park employees so that in case of an accident, they will notify the proper people, understand any special responsibilities, and take proper actions.

The first objective of the emergency plan should be the safety and protection of park visitors and employees, including providing immediate assistance to injured individuals and removing others from danger. The next objectives should be to protect property and to preserve or restore park services, operations, and programs. These directions should be reviewed and updated regularly.

5. Using accident reports for guidance Accident report forms should document necessary facts about each accident, obtain names and addresses of witnesses, and provide a basis for a follow-up investigation to determine the cause of the accident. The function of the investigation is not to determine fault, but to guide management in future park safety planning and risk management.

Together, these practices form the basis of a professional standard of care for the safety of visitors to parks and recreation facilities. If used effectively, these practices can help park departments see that neither accidents nor lawsuits "just happen."

PART 5

New
Directions

Managing
Leisure Services
in an Era
of Change

Joseph J. Bannon

Leisure services administrators must be able to withstand enormous conflicts and pressures. This prospect poses more than a dilemma for managers; it represents the ongoing reality of managing infinite uncertainty. Apart from cataclysms, the next few decades will undoubtedly see the culmination of many issues raised in recent decades, as well as the emergence of other issues barely evident now. Those issues will affect park and recreation administrators, just as they affect other organizations and institutions, public and private. The provision of leisure services, generally considered a positive cultural component in an advanced society, in no way frees our profession from the confusion of social, political, technological, and ethical pressures brought to bear on most organizations these days. It is naive to believe that a public agency can avoid the political and monetary pressures private enterprise faces. In many ways, our direct accountability to taxpayers puts us continually in the limelight.

Change is common to people, particularly in industrialized, competitive societies. Environmental, financial, social, and technological challenges have been with us for decades, and the leadership qualities needed to manage organizations in transition must include at least comprehension of these broad issues. To successfully administer an organization, an administrator must possess the following attributes:

1. Excel in organizational and interpersonal communications, reflecting a humanistic approach to administration. The

This article is excerpted from "Public Administration: Roots and Implications of Change," in Thomas L. Goodale and Peter W. Witt, eds., *Recreation and Leisure: Issues in an Era of Change,*" rev. ed. © 1985 by Venture Publishing, State College, PA. Reprinted with permission.

scope of these skills includes the necessity for creating work-places that stimulate individual motivation. It is a waste of an administrator's time to ceaselessly motivate others. Through effective, empathetic communication skills, an administrator should counsel, coach, and inspire others to undertake their own self-development, as well as ensure a work environment that in no way opposes or contradicts more humanistic values.

2. Be a scientific administrator, using accountability systems such as PERT, Management-by-Objectives, Zero-Base Budget-ing, systems analysis, or other managerial models and pro-grams. These management and accountability systems are integrated with and rely on computers and other automated devices. Parks and recreation professionals should not avoid these systems on the assumption that our organizations are too simple or small. In a time of increased accountability, the more sophisticated and accurate our planning and record-keeping systems, the greater the chances for improved per-formance in the face of reduced resources.

3. Possess a broad, eclectic intellectuality, not simply technical or administrative. Although technology and automated sys-tems are important, administrators should avoid becoming enamored of hardware. An administrator should obtain an overall knowledge of equipment and systems in an organiza-tion without gaining a specialist's or technician's comprehen-sion of these technologies. The tendency to become an administrative technician should be avoided, as knowledge of machines often draws one away from concern with people, a prime administrative task.

4. Recognize that what was once considered long range must be treated in shorter segments. There is nothing sacred about a 20-year span, especially when a few years can dramatically undermine any analysis with unexpected change. If forecast-ing is to be more meaningful, administrators must limit their time horizons, while at the same time expanding their imagi-native and speculative viewpoints.

5. Be proficient in the use of evaluation techniques for staff and service performance, which are necessary for accountability and productivity assessments. The literature on evaluation research methods has grown steadily during the past 20 years, offering administrators systematic programs for ap-praising an organization's internal and external performance. An administrator need no longer rely on intuition or personal judgment in measuring an employee's ability or a service. Such personal assessments are both arbitrary and subject to poor judgment. They are also subject to challenge, legally and

otherwise. Evaluation and accountability, especially in public organizations, go hand in hand. The more select and controlled the evaluation methods, the more likely administrators will avoid conflict with any emergent new work values, or a quality-conscious, resource-limiting public.

6. Contribute to and encourage original research in leisure behavior, reducing conflicts between theory and practice in parks and recreation. For the most part, recreation and parks literature is derivative or secondary, drawing on sociology, psychology, business administration, information science, economics, and marketing. While secondary data are not, in themselves, second rate, there is a clear need for encouraging intellectual leadership and creativity in leisure research.

The logical focus for such research is within the profession itself, drawing on rather than relying so heavily on other disciplines. To bridge the gap between academics and practitioners, we need skillful and tactful interpreters of research. The snobbery of the intellectual and the myopia of the hands-on practitioner have no place in a progressive organization.

As opportunities for leisure grow, our profession will be called upon to assess the phenomenon of people's diverse responses to more discretionary time. Currently we follow rather than lead in the analyses of leisure behavior. For instance, the popular press is ahead of us in such analyses, whereas in most other disciplines, popularization of ideas follows rigorous research and experience.

The most necessary skills during any transitional period are adaptive behavior and innovation. During these years of resource constraint, what is immeasurably important as everything shrinks is that our imaginations expand. While there are limited funds for traditional services and programs, it is surprising how much money is available to support new and innovative approaches. Unfortunately, many of these ideas and proposals are coming from private businesses and private contracts, or from administrators and employees who desert public agencies for the more lucrative atmosphere of private enterprise. Thus, the need for imagination and innovation in the face of change cannot be over-stressed.

For this purpose, an historical and intellectual perspective are both essential for effective, adaptive behavior. To understand what is happening at any point in time, one has to comprehend what has happened before, what has led up to, brought about, or even caused circumstances to change or evolve. Comprehension is an intellectual habit, best acquired in youth, and invaluable in an administrator. Nothing happens in a vacuum, but is related and interrelated to a variety of factors and circumstances that must be intellectually and personally perceived. It is not enough to accept what others posit as causes, as much as to determine these for oneself, or at least to go beyond the rhetoric of simplistic analyses or rationales that might be forthcoming. Although political realities are unavoidable, the larger constraint that parks and recreation faces as a profession is broader than politics, involving an ecological and ethical framework that takes us beyond self-interest and reactionary fear, that seeks to avoid anxiety, defensiveness or political conservatism. Change is inevitable, a form of temporal evolution essential to any vital existence. We should not regret what time has brought to bear, but rather confront the realities of the present day with the weight of history ever in mind, an inspiring burden in many ways if one has taken a proper measure of the centuries; taken the time, that is, to comprehend the forces of change in one's own time.

Managing Our Way to a Preferred Future

David Gray

This is a time of great concern, uncertainty, ambivalence, and ambiguity in the recreation and park movement. It is a time of change.

Even change is ambiguous. Some of it is subtle. It comes like a rising tide that is unrecognized until feet are wet. The full import may be known only in retrospect.

Change brings crisis *and* opportunity. In periods of rapid change, reforms are possible that could never be accomplished in periods of stability. Flexibility, recognition of opportunity, escape from pessimistic thinking, and leadership are required to respond to this period. Now is the time to escape yesterday's success and bring our dreams into reality.

In human affairs, the dream always precedes reality. What cannot be dreamed cannot be done. In the recreation and park movement, we need a new dream that is not an extension of the past but an expression of our future. Our new dream will precede our new reality. What we must dream is a vision of our preferred future. Realizing that dream will take planning, pathfinding, problem solving, and implementation.

At the 1983 Congress for Recreation and Parks, Kansas City, MO, the National Recreation and Park Association focused the attention of delegates on *Megatrends*, which may be the most significant act of the last decade in the life of the association. The potential significance for the cities, counties, and agencies the delegates represented is even higher *if* a process can be initiated that can link the broad environmental scan provided by the review of megatrends to

Reprinted from the May 1984 issue of *Parks & Recreation* by special permission of the National Recreation and Park Association..

the daily actions in the separate jurisdictions. That process is strategic planning.

On the whole, Americans have not been effective planners, especially large-scale, long-range planners. Our political orientation has rejected the concentration of planning activities in the hands of an intellectual elite. Our bias for action has created impatience with lengthy planning processes. Our commitment to short-range results, even at the expense of long-range gain, has created a climate in which planning has not been valued. The situation is beginning to change.

Our interest in planning has been renewed because of the realization that our traditional approaches to planning cannot sustain our leadership in the competition for international markets. In addition, dynamic social, political, economic, and technological environments have invalidated most of our assumptions about the future as an extension of the past. New planning approaches are based on wide participation and visions of a preferred future. There is a growing national commitment to strategic planning in both the private and public sectors.

In its simplest form, strategic planning consists of an environmental scan to identify major trends, issues, problems, and opportunities; identification of a preferred future for the agency; an audit of the agency's resources to identify strengths and weaknesses; formulation of strategies to attain the preferred future; and implementation of the strategies. This process of identifying a preferred future and working backward to design strategies to achieve it is a substantial departure from traditional planning.

Application of strategic planning in public organizations raises some critical questions that are not common in private organizations: Who should be involved in the process? How can priority questions be resolved in the absence of the "bottom line" considerations that aid private companies in reaching these decisions?

The short answer on involvement is that all those who can contribute to the planning process and to implementation of the plan when goals are clear should participate. Priority decisions are, in the end, subjective, but the strategic planning process clarifies the issues and relates decisions and actions to specific goals. This approach is often better than one in which decisions are reached solely on the basis of political power. It is difficult to see how communities and agencies can deal with environmental change, respond to their constituencies, and maintain their equilibrium without a strategic plan.

In the current wide-ranging debate on the quality of American management, a useful formulation characterizes the functions of management as pathfinding, problem solving, and implementation. In this country, we have concentrated on problem solving by making it quantitative, using systems methods, and trying to make management into a science. Analysis, the primary intellectual approach, is frequently carried out by personnel in staff assignments.

Implementation is managed by line officers working in an environment of collective bargaining agreements, close-up human relationships, conflict, production schedules, and organization politics. They approach the work more intuitively than analytically.

Pathfinding, as the word implies, is a kind of visionary leadership that can bring the organization through the kind of uncertain period we are in. It may exist anywhere in the organization, but it is most apt to occur, if it occurs at all, in the executive suite.

Executives have an institutional view, broader sources of information, an environmental scan, and wide contacts with interior and exterior publics. When these essential elements are combined with an intuitive mind and the ability to synthesize a broad picture, pathfinding can take place. Organizations with these ingredients are fortunate. Pathfinders are in short supply.

Some organizations are bureaucratic. They abhor surprises, control initiative, and punish failure. They reduce everything to a routine and establish rules and stay in their comfort zone. These entities operate on tight role prescriptions, organize on hierarchical principles, and concentrate authority at the top. They are devoted to efficiency. Their budgets are meticulous; there is great difficulty in financing even a mild departure from traditions.

The employee suggestion rate is minimal. There is a long institutional memory backed up by a strong culture that resists change and fosters stability. Few people look at the whole organization; they plan by updating the past. They have a hard time getting over yesterday's success. The bureaucratic organization focuses inward.

In contrast, entrepreneurial organizations support reasonable risk taking, learn from failure, and reward success. They do not punish failure. They realize that change creates opportunity and maintain an environmental scan to assess where opportunity exists. These groups work at the growing edge of practice in their field, bring collective intelligence to new ventures, and identify risk capital.

Many of their members are out of their organizational boxes, looking at the whole agency and making multiple suggestions for improvement. They tolerate ambiguity, encourage intuitive pathfindings, and look outward. They plan by working back from a preferred future. They honor their traditions, but are not bound by them.

These descriptions are stereotypes. Organizations rarely exist in pure bureaucratic or entrepreneurial form. But central tendencies are clear. In the public sector, there are far more bureaucratic than entrepreneurial agencies. Bureaucratic organizations do not prosper in times of dramatic change. The pathfinding challenge in public organizations is to find a way to overcome inertia, to permit reasonable risk taking, and to escape tradition. That is the challenge before us. To maintain our organizations and improve our services it may be necessary to adjust to the emerging paradigm of recreation agencies.

All social movements operate on a set of assumptions about reality that regulate their existence. The academic term for this set of assumptions is paradigm, which is essentially a model. A paradigm is an organization principle that governs perception, determines large areas of experience, points up what facts should be gathered, limits approaches to problem solving, suggests what solutions are acceptable, and selects the methods used to justify belief.

A paradigm is a powerful model that gives stability to social movements and provides guidelines for operations. It now appears that the recreaton movement is in the midst of what Thomas Kuhn (*Structure of Scientific Revolutions*) identified as a "paradigm shift." Figure 1 compares the traditional paradigm and the new model.

The traditional paradigm assumes that public recreation agencies will:	The new paradigm assumes that public recreation agencies will:
Provide equal services to all the citizens.	Provide services based on social and economic need.
Provide programs consisting of a series of activities selected from a restricted list of recreation pursuits.	Provide programs of human service that may go far beyond traditional recreation activities.
Act as a direct service provider.	Act as a community organizer and catalyst in matching community resources to citizen need.
Offer programs in department facilities.	Offer programs anywhere in the community.
Provide staff leadership of the activities.	Use staff resources to coach citizens until they can provide their own leadership.
Fund basic services from tax sources.	Fund services from a variety of sources, including fee-for-service, donations, sale of services, contract arrangements, barter, agency partnerships, and cooperation with the private sector, as well as tax resources.

Figure 1. Old and new paradigms for public recreation agencies.

The long domination of the traditional paradigm, which has governed most of our thinking and operations for about 50 years in public recreation, is now challenged by an emerging paradigm with a new set of assumptions about the nature of reality.

The emerging paradigm has not been created by service providers as an act of free will. Much of it has not come from service providers at all. It embodies a changed set of assumptions of such depth and scope that they are *very* threatening to the traditionalists among us. The emerging paradigm is born of social, economic, and political change. It is a survival strategy and a vision of service improvement that responds to recent setbacks the recreation and park movement has suffered in the strained political environment, the competition for public funds, and the need to cope with the great social changes occurring throughout the world.

Whether the new paradigm will govern our future thinking and operations no one can say now. Kuhn's description of the paradigm shift process suggests that old theory is never replaced by criticism alone. Traditional agencies will continue to assume the myth of coherence in the current model as long as they can. The crisis will

The traditional paradigm assumes that public recreation agencies will:	The new paradigm assumes that public recreation agencies will:
Plan by up-dating the past.	Plan by anticipating a preferred future, organizing services around client groups in response to participants' felt needs and a careful community-wide needs analysis.
Plan programs with the staff.	Plan with potential clients, community informants, other agencies, political figures, and corporations, as well as with staff.
Encourage participation by publicity.	Develop a marketing approach to operations.
Evaluate results primarily in terms of attendance.	Evaluate services in terms of human consequences.
Motivate the staff to work *for* the people.	Motivate the staff to work *with* the people.
Justify budgets in terms of historical precedent.	Justify budgets in terms of social need and program results.
Require financial accountability.	Require financial and program accountability.
Achieve the ultimate goals of a fine recreation program.	Achieve the ultimate goal of human development and community organization.

Figure 1—continued.

come when environmental change makes it more and more difficult to adapt the old model to the new conditions. For an increasing number of agencies, that crisis is here now.

Taken together, the elements of environmental scanning, identification of a preferred future, strategic planning, and path-findings, problem solving, and implementation provide a planning and operational process of great power. When this process is combined with recognition of the need for development of an entrepreneurial organization and commitment to the role changes implied by the emerging paradigm, we are capable of managing our way to a preferred future.

The Interactive Leader

Frank Benest, Jack Foley, and George Welton

If we are to transform the "crisis" of change into the "opportunity" of change, we will need organizations that empower their members, promote autonomy, and require interdependence. We must look at the quality of our thinking and the quality of our leadership. We must begin at the beginning, the quality of our thinking and the quality of our leadership, for they determine an organization culture, which, in turn, determines the level of innovation, trust, and entrepreneurship in any organization.

Calculative and meditative thinking

As professionals we have two ways of thinking, and each way influences our view of leadership. One way is called *calculative* and the other way is called *meditative* thinking. Calculative thought emphasizes the world of analysis, observation, and recording, while meditative thought contemplates "essence" and importance. It is meditative thought that guides and justifies calculative thought. This is as it should be, but not as it is.

Unfortunately, when we are overwhelmed by concern, uncertainty, ambivalence, and ambiguity, meditative thinking is sacrificed for calculative thinking, creating inactive leadership, typified by the bureaucratic functionary who is primarily concerned with the efficient and smooth functioning of the organization. The inactive leader is preoccupied with formalizing rules, implementing new technologies, and entrenching a rigid organizational structure. This kind of recreation manager produces efficiency, conformity, and

Reprinted from the November 1985 issue of *Parks & Recreation* by special permission of the National Recreation and Park Association. This article was originally entitled "Managing Our Way to a Preferred Future ... Continued."

regularity through precise adherence to procedures. Eventually everyone, superiors and subordinates, becomes trapped in an arena where there is no need to think creatively. Workers act in the "normal" way. The working day is the ordinary day. Mediocracy prevails. Actions become institutionalized. And, during times of change, "crisis" sets in.

To turn crisis into opportunity, leaders must think meditatively. Such thinking produces the interactive leader, who is the opposite of the inactive leader. In comparison to the inactive leader, the interactive leader is usually considered a revolutionary and non-conformist who deviates from the status quo. The interactive leader seeks change rather than ignores it, encourages colleagues to exercise individual creativity rather than succumb to structured regularity, and actively places human and community concerns first rather than institutional concerns. And, in times of change, problems, concerns, and even crisis are perceived as opportunities that can be seized for the benefit of all.

Organizational culture

The difference between inactive and interactive leadership is reflective of an organization's culture, its values, myths, and symbols. Culture is the spirit, soul, and heart of an organization. It influences the entire organization. Organizational culture "affects practically everything—from who gets promoted and how decisions are made to how employees dress and what sports they play." (Quoted from "Corporate Cultures—The Rites and Rituals of Corporate Life," *Los Angeles Times*, Aug. 20, 1982.)

The organizational culture created by inactive leadership has no clear values or beliefs about how to succeed and results in low morale and wasted energy. It is a "rule centered" culture and seeks the appearance of efficiency with rules covering dress, work hours, coffee breaks, performance, and productivity.

On the other hand, in the culture created by interactive leadership, everyone knows the goals of the organization and works to achieve them. These cultures are "goal-centered" in which workers agree on goals and share a sense of commitment and purpose. The staff feels secure to pursue both innovation and entrepreneurship. People in this kind of vibrant culture are not satisfied with simply maintaining services; they understand change is inevitable. And in today's world, change has accelerated beyond anything known before, making innovation a measure of success.

For a long time many recreation and park agencies have misdirected resources to unproductive and obsolete programs that no longer serve a viable community need or social purpose. For example, an agency may continue to offer an annual boys basketball tournament in a community that has undergone demographic changes and is now composed of predominantly Hispanic residents who prefer soccer. Tiny tots programs, which provide social and cultural activities to help children adapt to school, do not meet the needs of single working parents with pre-school and school-aged children.

If an agency is to be innovative, it must organize itself to abandon the old, the obsolete, and the unproductive. In the private sector, competition and the profit motive force organizations to give up obsolete products. But public and non-profit sectors do not have such bottom line measures and, thus, are especially vulnerable to obsolescence. For an organization to shed the obsolete and begin to innovate, it must continuously generate ideas, involve and support certain kinds of individuals who have a propensity for change and innovation, and provide a structure conducive for new enterprises.

Innovation starts with an idea. Ideas are born small, immature, and shapeless. They are promises rather than fulfillment. In an innovative agency, no idea is put down. Since few ideas survive, leaders demand that they be thought through in terms of the work needed to turn the idea into a service, a process, a business, or a technology. In confronting a new idea, the interactive leader asks: "What's to be done and what's to be learned before we can commit ourselves and our resources to this idea?"

Innovators

People who can implement new ideas are called innovators. These people share a number of characteristics, as do the organizations in which innovation flourishes. According to Rosabeth Moss Kanter in "The Middle Manager as Innovator," *Harvard Business Review*, July-Aug. 1982:

They are comfortable with change, trust that uncertainties will be clarified, and view unmet needs as opportunities.

They have clarity of direction and long-range horizons that help them see setbacks as only temporary.

They are thorough in preparing for meetings and presentations, and they cultivate a sense of who can help them in the organization.

They have a participative management style, encouraging subordinates' efforts, promising rewards, and keeping their promises.

They are persistent and persuasive, knowing that successes do not come overnight, but through perseverance.

It is the task of the interactive leader to develop innovators and innovation. However, innovation can only be promoted in a culture characterized by a shared sense of trust. Trust is important because, without it, one is afraid to take on the risk involved in changing and growing. It is the catalyst for change. When trust is high, persons and social systems change naturally in beneficial ways. Trust enhances the flow of mental processes. In his work on integrating the individual and the organization, Chris Argyris noted that removal of fear and the development of trust are essential for "psychic successes." (*Integrating the Individual and the Organization*, 1982.) Psychic energy increases as one experiences psychic success and decreases with psychic failure.

Argyris cites two requirements for trust to replace fear: the individual must value himself and aspire to experience an increasing sense of competence; and the person must increase awareness and acceptance of self and others. With trust, psychic energy is increased and mobilized, creativity is heightened, people act in more direct and effective ways, and the whole organization benefits. An organizational culture that is trustworthy and promotes innovation also encourages entrepreneurship.

The new entrepreneurship

In isolated situations, during these changing times in leisure and human services, we see a flourishing of "new entrepreneurship." While the term is often bandied around, what exactly is this new entrepreneurship? Basically, it involves agency leaders, acting alone or with partners, who seek and seize new opportunities to deliver services in unorthodox ways to existing or new clients—and to generate the revenue to pay for their effort.

Some examples include the following:

Agencies like the Human Services Department in Gardena, CA, have repackaged traditional services, identified new program benefits attractive to private companies, and marketed the programs for a fee to local employers. Such services include child care services for employees of local firms, English-As-a-Second-Language in the factory programs, supervisory training, and drug and alcohol abuse services.

Some cities and counties, such as San Francisco and Los Angeles County, and special districts, such as the East Bay Park and Recreation District in Oakland, CA, have developed fund-raising foundations that apply for corporate grants, solicit civic contributions, and conduct fund-raising special events.

The City of San Diego, San Ramon Public Utilities District in California, and the City of Edmonton in Alberta, Canada, have created non-profit community foundations or use existing ones to operate facilities and conduct programs. Local governments partially subsidize these "operating" foundations, which also raise outside funds or match the government grant with "sweat equity."

Where there is a high demand for new residential or commercial development, yet limited space, cities like San Francisco and

Santa Monica have insisted that developers either create services or pay in-lieu fees to fund new programs such as affordable housing, child care, parks, or cultural arts.

Public agencies have been successful in negotiating with the private sector for the use of non-cash resources in meeting community needs. The City of Baltimore negotiated with John Hopkins University Hospital to establish a health services project at senior citizen housing projects. Cities across the nation have involved businesses and labor unions in providing free materials, equipment, and services to rehabilitate housing structures as shelters for the homeless. The Hillsborough County, MN, Department of Aging Services negotiated with Honeywell to use its cars during non-peak hours to transport the elderly to nutrition sites and senior centers. And, senior programs throughout California have involved merchants to sell services and merchandise to the elderly at 10-20 percent discounts as part of the Golden State Discount Program.

Characteristics of entrepreneurs

Who are the entrepreneurs who initiate these new schemes to develop the support and funding to better serve people? Entrepreneurs are those who work for themselves. They are people who want control of their lives, to be more than wage earners. They see themselves as making things happen rather than waiting for things to happen. To be successful, parks and recreation professionals must be entrepreneurs in the sense that they actively work to bring about change, to make things happen, and to create a better world. Entrepreneurs feel "unfamiliar" with the usual work setting. They prefer risk over safety. In parks and recreation, the entrepreneur is willing to risk security and to some extent the agency rather than perpetuate tradition. There are three dominant personality traits of the entrepreneur:

1. *Locus of control.* This means they feel they influence the course of events. They are in charge of their personal events.
2. *Independence.* They do not see themselves as having a "boss." They work for themselves.
3. *Imagination.* This is important in that entrepreneurs must be able to see themselves as successful in their projected ventures. They must feel what they are attempting is credible.

Based upon these traits, entrepreneurs display certain characteristics. Ted Gaebler ("The Entrepreneurial Manager," *Public Management*, 1983) has listed six:

1. Goal oriented, not task oriented
2. Flexible

3.   Willing to take calculated risks

4.   Profit-oriented

5.   Future oriented

6.   Create a sense of ownership for themselves.

While many professionals may not exhibit all these entrepreneurial qualities, they may have entrepreneurial potential. All they lack are the proper incentives. Thus, an entrepreneur can often be "discovered." That is, through interactive leadership, the conditions can be created within an organizational culture that encourage the entrepreneur to come forward. The responsibility of the leader is not limited to hiring people with entrepreneurial qualities but includes providing the conditions that promote entrepreneurship. Entrepreneurs thrive in those organizations whose culture has a sense of aliveness. Employees are optimistic about the future because they know that they are making things happen. They see change as an opportunity to continue working toward their goals or ideals.

Agency leaders must legitimize entrepreneurship among their workers. To do so, leaders must promote an atmosphere of freedom and creativity. New ideas need to be supported, work hours need to be flexible, and agency resources need to be available. Employees cannot feel dependent and controlled. Yet, legitimacy goes beyond simply arranging for support; superiors must be willing to "get involved." They must take an active interest in the workers' projects. There should be periodic progress reports, frequent problem-solving discussion, and sincere commitment to improving the quality of work life as well as community life.

As we step back and look at all that has been said in this article, it seems overwhelming. How can we as professionals live up to these standards? Are they realistic? Certainly none of us is the perfect leader and no organization is the perfect organization. In fact, most of us would acknowledge that there can probably never be the perfect leader or the perfect organization, but that does not mean that we cannot try. Perhaps it is more reasonable that interactive leadership—with its attendant trust, innovation, and entrepreneurship—be a goal for us all.

"Grass Roots" Community Development of Leisure Opportunity

J. P. Tindell

The process of "community development" has taken on many meanings and served many purposes since its beginnings in the 1950s. In its most organized form, it has been referred to as "neighborhoodism" and the "national neighborhood movement." Schwartz (1979:9) perhaps best describes it as a movement that "aims to establish personal ties among the residents of specific areas of cities in the hope of combatting the impersonal character of urban life and of finding a basis for community that transcends [other] considerations." This definition emphasizes a concern for the general quality of community life that can be enhanced by efforts to bring people together. It is to this same end—that of a personally meaningful and high-quality lifestyle for all—that the leisure experience, as one of many positive human experiences, can contribute.

Providing opportunities for people to get together to fulfill socialization needs and achieve community goals can have important economic, educational, political, and individual ramifications as well. Community development may embody a myriad of processes and activities, depending on the needs of a particular group of people. Biddle (1965:282) documents the wide range of purposes, goals, and meanings that are a part of this concept. They range from ensuring quality services for all people and raising the economic levels of residents and local businesses to educating and organizing in order to bring pressure on the more powerful in order to gain certain rights and privileges. As part of the individual human growth process, community development can serve as a "means for develop-

From the *Journal of Park and Recreation Administration* 2, no. 1 (January 1984). Reprinted with permission from the Academy of Park and Recreation Administration.

ing people to higher levels of cooperative competence, an actualization of good personal potentials through the experience of working together" (Biddle 1965:282).

Schwartz (1979:10) further describes the neighborhood movement as having among its goals the following:

1. Creating social cohesion within neighborhood communities
2. Establishing economic reciprocity between citizens of a city and the public and private institutions to which they contribute
3. Achieving administrative efficiency and responsiveness in delivery of municipal services
4. Broadening democratic participation in urban political parties and voluntary associations
5. Building strategies and action for neighborhood improvement and empowerment
6. Providing an avenue for democratic participation.

Goering (1979) states that neighborhood development organizations frequently have been the principal instruments for the improvement, development, revitalization, stabilization, and renewal of cities.

The burgeoning of social service programs in the 1930s was a result of the Depression, and was intended to help rebuild and maintain a certain quality of life. These "New Deal" programs continued to proliferate as the U.S. economy grew stronger. Funds became available to update older, declining communities through renewal programs. In response to the human impact of this governmental intrusion, however, groups of people organized to oppose their exclusion from the decision-making behind the proposed demolition and rebuilding of their neighborhoods. Another government program that proved ill-conceived was the "War on Poverty" in the 1960s. Although it attempted to provide resources to depressed areas to assist with improvements, the proposed recipients of assistance rarely had a voice in determining specific uses of allocated funds. Programs dictated from afar, therefore, too often did not meet real needs, and treated the symptoms as opposed to the real causes of local community problems.

Present trends in community development movements reflect an increased dominance of the idea of public ownership, a more socialistic approach to solving collective problems. Government has recently realized the necessity of "grass-roots" participation in the planning and administration of improvement efforts. The Community Development Block Grant and Neighborhood Self-Help Development programs of the 1970s now provide grants and other assistance to groups for self-help projects that require private citizen participation in all aspects. This redirection of resources is highlighted by Bannon (1973:39). He speaks of the change from "helping society's maladjusted adapt" to altering those aspects of society that injure the human spirit: "We will not produce any real or lasting results in community work until the focus of our work shifts from the objects of change (the poor) to the agents of change, and the settings in which change can occur." Kotler (1979) observes the "state of the art" in community development to be a mixture of advocacy, service delivery, and development as the present goals of neighborhood associations. One can see as well the potential these processes have for enhancing the total human development process for individuals while at the same time instilling a sense of civic responsibility for overall community welfare and quality of life.

Problems of modern-day living

A scrutiny of present-day American life reveals circumstances that set the stage for the continued evolution of citizen advocacy groups. For example, limited public financial resources necessitate alternative ways of maintaining services with decreased governmental support. Ethnically diverse populations demand maintenance of their cultural integrity, such that services must be tailored to special needs and values. The tendency of increasingly automated employment environments and high population mobility to create experiences of remoteness, isolation, and impersonality in daily living and social relationships motivates a renewed reaching out to others to reclaim a sense of caring and belonging. The frustrations and pressures created by dense populations, limited open space, and high unemployment likewise contribute to feeling "locked in" to a cycle of mere survival for many. Individual and collective feelings of power and influence over one's destiny continue to disintegrate. A crisis involving loss of identity and enforced leisure has developed for groups that cannot fully participate as valued workers and conspicuous consumers in American society.

The direct involvement of citizens in providing for their community's needs at a grass-roots level can heighten personal growth and development or provide a special avenue for "disenfranchised" persons to build the positive self-image necessary to mental health and spiritual vitality by enabling the participation of citizens in creating their own destinies. Human service agencies can help fulfill this need for self-determination and personal power and can provide opportunities for people to commit themselves to meeting their own needs and those of their neighbors as well.

In a discussion of the implications of the holistic perspective on leisure, Murphy (1974:227) says that "the central focus of leisure service should be *encouraging individual initiative and choice.*" This perspective, and the pressured conditions present in American life, call for a direct response on the part of park and recreation agencies to the *total* realm of real human needs, including the opportunity for leisure expression and experience.

Leisure in American life

A study by Green (1978) showed that community organizations and action programs throughout the U.S. considered the issue of recreation a high priority for their attention, ranking it eighth among forty. Other generally accepted values placed on the benefits of leisure to the individual and the community form the basis for the leisure service profession as a whole. Some of these inherent values include the following:

1. Availability of open space for unrestrained movement and exploration
2. Heightened individual and collective human growth and development
3. Contribution to a positive self-concept
4. Satisfaction of personal needs for self-expression and creativity
5. Opportunities for "building community" (social bonding)
6. Evolution of independent functioning.

Given the above discussion about some of the pressures of living in modern society, it would seem critically important to do whatever it takes to safeguard opportunities for leisure and to provide it in the future by expanding the involvement of the individual in ensuring that it is available in his or her own community.

Citizen involvement in leisure opportunity development

Making private citizens fuller partners in the provision of leisure opportunities has become a necessity. Public park and recreation departments would be wise to explore the application of community development techniques in establishing mechanisms by which citizens can assume increased responsibility for meeting their own leisure needs. The forms that this evolution of "people empowerment" takes need be limited only by the creativity of its initiators. It has exciting possibilities because of its potential for contributing to the development of responsible, concerned citizens actively involved in both creating and maintaining access to leisure resources for themselves within their immediate communities.

Community development is a process that can provide public parks and recreation agencies with financial and human resources to assist with ongoing program and facility operations. These resources can include participation in park maintenance or program administration and can take the form of special citizen action or advisory councils, neighborhood associations, park stewardship committees, or "Friends of the Park" groups. In addition to operational support, the active recruitment, training, and supervision of people from the private sector make a valuable contribution to building community. Opportunities for leisure activities at a nearby park site can be a dynamic means for the actualization of human potential and cooperative accomplishment. Some specific outcomes of this citizen involvement process might include: community projects for the prevention of crime and vandalism in parks, community gardening projects, community pride programs, neighborhood cultural arts celebrations, and youth development clubs.

Community development in San Jose, California: A case study

Serious urban problems—crime, vandalism, youth violence, truancy, unemployment, and low income—had reached a crisis point in downtown San Jose in 1980. City and county school administrators and law enforcement officials began meeting with concerned community leaders, and the "Si Se Puede" (It Can Be Done) Project was born. Originally funded by the city of San Jose, the Santa Clara County Office of Education, and the Mott Foundation, the project is administered by the County Education Office's Community Education Center. Since its inception, numerous area foundations and corporations have supported this effort to alleviate youth violence and school absenteeism. Another pivotal goal is the improvement of the self-image of young people and of the general welfare and health conditions of the neighborhoods within a 300-square block area that is heavily Hispanic and has growing concentrations of Indochinese and Portuguese people.

A multidisciplinary approach involving all key area agencies in supporting local residents in creating cooperative solutions to area problems has been used. The project's management team includes heads of San Jose's Police and Parks and Recreation Departments, the Mexican-American Community Services Agency, Mosquitos Eastside Action Club, and the Black Council of Santa Clara County. This team meets regularly for collective planning and decision-making. The high-level participation of the Parks and Recreation Department in the project's management acknowledges the importance of open space and positive leisure activities in regenerating the vitality and enhancing the quality of life in the project's service area.

Enthusiastic cooperation among project staff, residents, and community organizations has generated a broad spectrum of activities and programs as solutions to area problems. Project staff Community School Workers (CSWs) do home visits, provide informal counseling for "problem" students, work with juvenile offenders and their probation officers, and coordinate with school personnel, parks and recreation staff, and others to provide community cultural events and recreation opportunities. As an indication of commitment to public service, interdisciplinary teams of student interns (including recreation majors) from San Jose State University work with CSWs at each of the target area's schools. New Games festivals, neighborhood cleanups, dances, and holiday fairs take place in schools, parks, libraries, and on the streets of the area, giving various ethnic groups and persons of all ages opportunities to interact positively.

The project's specific community development objectives require staff to meet with residents and serve as resources for community councils. Councils are assisted in identifying community problems and in developing and implementing plans of action to address them with the full cooperation and support of local human service professionals. Skills in conducting community meetings and community organizing are developed at citizen action training workshops.[1]

Further implications for the park and recreation professional

Fuller participation in generating holistic solutions to community problems has its place among the responsibilities of leisure service professionals. Limited public funds necessitate an approach different from directly serving constituents. Park and recreation resources—facilities and staff—should be fully utilized in cooperative problem-solving and programming with local agencies and residents. Solutions should incorporate creative alternatives for healthy, economically vital neighborhoods and a true sense of community—people working together to take responsibility for the quality of their environment. Park and recreation staff must continue to take responsibility for maintaining access to leisure experiences for citizens, often shifting from their previous role of direct providers to that of community catalysts/facilitators.

Citizen coalitions can be assisted with incorporating themselves as nonprofit, public benefit corporations to take over operations of community centers that local governments can no longer afford to support. City staff can then serve as trainers, consultants, and monitors of these new provider groups. Citizen groups can be used to do special fundraising and provide extensive voluntary support for maintaining public facilities by sponsoring "Adopt A Park," park cleanup, tree planting, and park watch programs.

Making the transition to the catalyst role will require special training for park and recreation staff. Skills to be developed include knowledge of formal and informal political processes; means of volunteer recruitment and management; how to establish nonprofit, public benefit corporations; citizen involvement/human motivation techniques; means of assessing community needs; ways of organizing neighborhood associations; group processes; conflict resolution/ mediation; strategic planning/problem solving; and citizen action training.[2]

Ensuring success: Realities and challenges

There is much to be learned to ensure the success of such an endeavor. The literature draws attention to the hard lessons learned in the past by "community developers."

A choice must be made about the exact role that citizen groups will take in relation to the funding source. Will the citizen group serve strictly as a voluntary service to the community, or will they be paid via a contractual agreement for their services, as a substitute for direct services previously provided by agency staff? And what new roles, then, must agency staff assume in relation to these citizen groups? Biddle (1965) outlines the broad spectrum of roles that can be assumed by community developers. They range from providing technical assistance and advice to taking an active posture as community organizers and catalysts. Choosing the appropriate role should depend on the needs of the citizenry, as opposed to the needs of the sponsoring agency. Agreements should clearly define each group's responsibilities and expectations, whether for funded or voluntary services.

Other realities of the community development process will affect the degree of success of such an endeavor. Human development in general is often a slow, subtle process with an unpredictable ebb and flow. A particular sensitivity to individual and group needs will be a requirement for the proper pacing of a group's efforts. Although, theoretically, the group process should involve the total community it serves, specialized interests very often become "squeaky wheels" demanding "oiling." And the numbers of persons active at any given time will often represent only a small fraction of the total population. Herein lies the challenge of motivating continuous participation where only a voluntary commitment is required of citizen participants.

The dilemma of making a choice between allegiance to "the people" or to "the establishment" will be critical as the needs of groups take on political import. Realistically, developing "savvy" of both formal and informal political processes will be a necessity, and is something that cannot be avoided if the professional intends to serve real human needs.

It is impossible to be politically neutral. We must understand that by not helping people define their needs and by not helping them to affect their own lives, we, in fact, are committing a political act, one that has devastating ramifications. In trying to remain politically neutral, recreators become politically neutered (Benest 1981:38).

Some classic conflicts have plagued the political success of community development efforts and reflect differences in perspective on the values and purposes of such work. Alinsky (1975) advocated active organizing for the purpose of gaining power through purposeful escalation of conflict and confrontation in order to sustain citizen commitment to issues and to force change. This tack is in direct contrast to "community focus" programs as led by Martin Luther King and Cesar Chavez. Rather than advocate pervasive change in "the system," this latter approach follows a gentler process, with group action governed by traditional ethical values of justice, reciprocity, responsibility, freedom, and fellowship. The community development movement has also encountered a paradox regarding autonomy. Within the present suprasystem, the cry for government decentralization and "grass roots" econo-political autonomy comes into conflict with reliance on national and local funding sources. The dilemma is in the fiscal dependency of groups on an entity whose intrusion into their lives has been the reason for their turning to self-advocacy (Schwartz 1979).

Documented shortcomings in a preponderance of social reform programs point historically to the difficulty of isolating the true causes from the mere symptoms of problems. Similarly, citizen action groups have repeatedly found that human energy is most easily rallied and maintained around a specific problem or issue (e.g., repaving streets, planning a new neighborhood park). The challenge for agency staff will be to employ principles of human motivation to keep people interested in and committed to a group's ongoing growth and operation.

In view of these realities, proven true by a wealth of successful and not-so-successful community organizations, the active commitment of park and recreation agencies to the principles of human development through citizen involvement in all aspects of planning, providing, and evaluating services is an undertaking that will require specialized training of professional staff. Tindell (1983) strongly advocates the development of training programs that build specific skills in citizen participation and community development processes.

Conclusion

Park and recreation professionals find themselves, then, immersed in generating sensitive responses to the leisure needs of their communities with fewer traditional resources than ever before. This problem, however, presents a rare opportunity to sow seeds of powerful personal growth through the redirecting of resources and skills, such that citizens identify and work to meet more of their own leisure and related human needs, supported and facilitated in this process by the trained professional. Park and recreation professionals must, then, begin to see themselves "as advocates of a quality and style of life, decided not by us, but rather by the people who live it" (Tindell 1983:2)—a life that professionals can build in constantly expanding partnership with citizen groups. The results of these new partnerships and roles will be a greatly heightened enrichment of leisure opportunity and quality of life for those willing to participate in creating vitalizing solutions to the challenges of community life.

Notes

1. Additional information about the "Si Se Puede" Project is available from: Community Education Center, Santa Clara County Schools, 100 Skyport Drive, San Jose, California 95115.

2. The San Jose Parks and Recreation Department has developed an annotated resource guide outlining the content and availability of various publications and organizations in California and the U.S. dealing with citizen participation/community development. The resources included cover the full spectrum of both theoretical and practical/implementation materials. *Community Development and Urban Leisure Opportunity: An Annotated Resource Guide* (1983) is available at a minimal cost from: Future Focus, P.O. Box 851, San Jose, California 95106-0851.

References

Alinsky, S. 1975. *Rules for radicals.* New York: Random House.

Bannon, J. 1973. Community outreach in recreation—We're coming after you. In *Outreach: Extending community service in urban areas,* edited by J. Bannon. Springfield, Ill.: Charles C. Thomas.

Benest, F. 1981. People organizing in a government context. In Department of Parks and Recreation, *Special report on human services.* Sacramento, Calif.: State of California Resources Agency.

Biddle, W. 1965. *The community development process: The rediscovery of local initiative.* New York: Holt, Rinehart and Winston.

Goering, J. 1979. The national neighborhood movement: A preliminary analysis and critique. *American Planning Association Journal* 45:506-14.

Green, G. 1978. *Who is organizing the neighborhood?* Washington, D.C.: Law Enforcement Assistance Administration.

Kotler, M. 1979. A public policy for neighborhood and community organizations. *Social Policy* 10:37-43.

Murphy, J. 1974. *Concepts of leisure: Philosophical implications.* Englewood Cliffs, N.J.: Prentice-Hall.

Schwartz, E. 1979. Neighborhoodism: A conflict of values. *Social Policy* 9:8-14.

Tindell, J. 1983. *Community development and urban leisure opportunity: A resource guide* (unpublished manuscript). San Jose, Calif.: Parks and Recreation Department.

Reassessing the Role of Public Leisure Services

H. Douglas Sessoms

For nearly eighty years, local park and recreation systems have served as the cornerstone of the park and recreation movement. Spawned by the conservation and social welfare reforms at the turn of the century and nurtured by federal programs during WWI and the Depression, local park and recreation systems became an accepted part of local government. By 1950, nearly every incorporated community of 10,000 or more in the United States had established a public recreation department or commission. The growth of professional organizations and formal programs for the education of professional park and recreation personnel has been directly related to the growth of local governmental services.

Early patterns shape current expectations

As is true of all social movements, the early approaches to the content and delivery of leisure services were based on the needs and technologies of the times. However, these early programs and organizational forms became the standard of what parks and recreation *should* be. Many of our current expectations of leisure services derive from earlier models, especially when those models were the experience base of those who now set policy. It is not surprising that Ronald Reagan, who grew up in a rural area at a time when voluntary associations were the primary approach to the provision of programs for youth, would strongly support voluntarism and the private financing of leisure services.

In analyzing the past, present, and future of local park and recreation systems, it is important to understand that a social mandate is what gives direction to a social movement. When the people enact legislation to create or support a program of services, they expect those services to fulfill their expectations, and they elect or employ persons to ensure that the mandate is carried out. The actions of government become its policies, and its policies direct its future actions. When government changes direction and services, it does so in response to new mandates. When government officials fail to meet the expectations of the public, that is, to fulfill the mandate, the public typically dismisses them or creates alternative structures to meet its needs.

Who are the clients for public recreation?
Public parks and recreation has always prided itself on its ability to provide services for all. In reality, its programs have been largely for the young, the athletic, and the underprivileged. However, during the 1960s and early 1970s, new program responsibilities were added as a result of select federal legislation and funds, especially those related to the acquisition and development of facilities and programs for special populations and the elderly. As specialized interest groups and the private recreation associations that they created to support their interests emerged, many of the traditional public programs (e.g., playgrounds, after-school programs, and teen centers) were regarded as no longer necessary and discontinued.

The growth of private recreation groups
An increasing number of neighborhood recreation associations developed throughout the 1970s, nearly all of which stressed the fact that club members could control their activities. Self-determination became increasingly important, even though the privilege of control was expensive. These independent recreation associations were often encouraged by local realtors, who saw the sale of the recreational lifestyle as a means of marketing real estate. Rarely did these associations have any relationship to the plans or operations of local park and recreation systems. Their presence, however, may have affected the level and types of public support for public systems, especially as two issues arose: (1) duplication and (2) the types of service the local departments were expected to provide.

Reassessing government's role
The issue came to a head in 1978, when California taxpayers enacted Proposition 13, which was intended to control growth by controlling the tax rate. Fueled by a new wave of social and political conservatism, Americans began to reassess the role of government and the relationship of government to the private sector. Government was viewed at all levels as being too large, too involved in the private lives of individuals, and too restrictive of free enterprise. Could not many of the programs and services of government be better handled by the private sector? Why should there be a local recreation and park agency when there were spas, private racquet and swim clubs,

amusement centers, employee recreation services, family entertainment (e.g., TV, computer games, VCRs) to do the job? How can parks and recreation serve those who see themselves and their private associations, not local public agencies, as the primary providers of recreation services?

Public recreation and the private-sector model   As a result of such changes, some politicians and public officials may no longer view parks and recreation as a public necessity, and some have suggested that the private sector is in a better position than government to respond to many of the public's recreation wishes and needs. According to this view, which is shared by some park and recreation professionals, the public prefers to pay for its recreational experiences directly, at the time of the experience, rather than to support recreation programs and services through general tax appropriations. Some park and recreation administrators now believe that they must adopt the entrepreneurial approach if their programs are to survive.

Recent park and recreation journals are filled with articles about entrepreneurial strategies, pricing strategies, and marketing techniques as applied to park and recreation services. University and college curricula have also assumed the validity of this viewpoint and instituted courses in marketing recreation and leisure services. The assumption that the private-sector model should be the primary means of supporting and delivering park and recreation services has potentially serious consequences, for it calls into question the social mandate for park and recreation systems and the role professionals are to assume in fulfilling the mandate.

Those who support a private-sector model for the provision of public recreation services cite several justifications.

First, they argue that the public has come to expect to pay for services rendered and that paying for the service at the time of the event gives the purchaser more control over the exchange and ultimately improves the quality of the service rendered. For the consumer, paying for services is an easy and quick way to monitor the value of the goods received.

Second, it is argued that although federal cutbacks may not directly affect the tax support for local recreation systems, they will affect it indirectly in the not-too-distant future. As local governments adjust to cuts in those areas where the federal government was once involved in support of local services, local officials will either have to increases taxes or reduce support for what they consider to be "nonessential" services. Some professionals in the field believe that parks and recreation may be in that category and would, therefore, experience budgetary cuts. By becoming more entrepreneurial and generating more support through direct pricing, park and recreation systems could assure themselves of adequate funds, and needed and desired services would not be reduced.

Third, some park and recreation professionals believe that local governmental services cannot compete with the private sector—that there is something inherently better in the private approach to services. Since the recreational experience is a personal, consumable experience, it logically falls into the private domain. However, if recreation is to be provided by the public sector, the content and delivery of services should closely mirror the private-sector approach.

Finally, there is the argument that since the majority of our citizens are now adults and older adults, the youth-oriented recreation approach of the past is dated and possibly irrelevant. Adults want and expect different services than they received as children and have formed private recreation groups to gain more control over their resources and activities. The current public-sector approach to service delivery does not take into account the expectations and needs of the adult population. Unless the public sector can offer the flexibility of the private sector—treating adults *as* adults—it cannot compete with the private sector for access to the adult market.

Accompanying these arguments for a more entrepreneurial approach to the provision of park and recreation services is a set of beliefs about the role of parks and recreation. One such belief is that the public sector is only a small element of the total local leisure service delivery system and that government should, therefore, be more concerned with facilities and facilitation than with direct programming. Rather than provide services directly, government should influence the private sector to provide direct services. Government should be the last resort in case the private sector is unable or unwilling to provide services. This view also holds that current public programs might be better managed if some public resources and programs were leased to the private sector. Or, rather than expand their own facilities and operations, the public sector could encourage the private sector to provide a set of quasi-public opportunities. For example, instead of building a new park, local recreation and park systems might use tax incentives to encourage large landholders to convert some of their property into "public" parks, thereby saving the public from having to make the capital expenditure for additional land acquisitions.

Interestingly, few supporters of such plans have asked whether the loss of tax revenue through tax incentives is outweighed by the gains accrued by not having to enact a bond issue. Which option is the least costly: reducing the tax payment for those who make a civic contribution, a loss that must be passed on to others, or enacting a bond issue that is paid for by all? In the final analysis, the public pays for both approaches.

Traditional financing of parks and recreation   The issues of who pays and which services are to be rendered are at the heart of the matter. Those who argue for the status quo, that is, for the continuation of the traditional approach to provision of local park and recreation services, have their points:

Supporters of the traditional approach strongly argue that public park and recreation programs came into being because of the inadequacies of the private, membership approach. They believe that the social mandate is still the same: that the public expects recreation and parks to be provided by government just as government provides education, streets and highways, and fire protection. The issue is not whether government should provide services but the type of services to be provided.

Second, supporters of the traditional approach argue that the public has made an enormous investment in parks and recreation: billions of dollars have been expended to acquire land and facilities. Since these were acquired in the name of the public and are held in public trust, the public has already paid for the resources, and government must continue to maintain these resources and make them available to the public free of charge.

The third argument is that extensive use of the entrepreneurial approach by local park and recreation systems will cause the public to expect the systems to be self-supporting. The hard-earned place of local park and recreation systems as an essential element of government would be lost—and difficult to regain, should the entrepreneurial approach fail to meet the public's needs and expectations. Granted that the entrepreneurial approach allows agencies more flexibility in responding to changing public interest, but this flexibility exacts a cost: it threatens the continuance of long-term investments and facilities and programs that have fluctuating or cyclical patterns of use.

Finally, critics of the entrepreneurial approach note that socially and economically disadvantaged individuals would experience even greater inequities if local park and recreation service systems were to rely extensively on the free-enterprise model. Persons with low incomes would be unable to purchase recreation opportunities or would be forced into the position of having to be declared "poor" in order to gain free or reduced admission to various activities and services. It is argued also that the private-sector model might negatively affect innovative programming, since numbers, rather than quality, would define "successful" programming. In many ways, the entrepreneurial approach expresses an elitist perspective: that "public" services are only for those who cannot provide for themselves. Such a viewpoint connects public recreation with a negative rather than a positive self-image; the risk is that having to rely upon public park and recreation agencies for leisure services will come to be equated with having to use food stamps to purchase groceries.

Finding a middle ground Fortunately, remaining with the status quo or totally embracing the entrepreneurial approach are not the only two alternatives for public recreation agencies. There are middle grounds, combinations of various approaches. The determining factor is the mandate: What does the public want and expect of its public recreation services?

Local park and recreation systems are a product of their past, of present conditions, and of thinking about the future. The most critical element in the success of a local system is the congruence between what the public wants and expects from its park and recreation system and the system's ability to meet those expectations. The expectations should be viewed in terms of (1) the services rendered and (2) the means by which those services are rendered. In other words, program content and organizational policies are equally important. If the public expects the local park and recreation system to provide programs free of charge, then a user fee policy would not be in the best interest of the system. If local residents see parks and recreation as primarily a service for low-income groups, whether they be the young or older adults, then it would be inappropriate for the park and recreation agency to implement entrepreneurial strategies. If the public expects parks and recreation to be self-supporting, then a "pay-as-you-go" approach is in order. Local agencies should not, however, change their program content or approach simply because the literature suggests that parks and recreation is dealing with new public expectations and attitudes. Imitation should not be the basis for programmatic and structural change.

Not all communities are changing at the same rate or in the same direction, nor do events in one state necessarily reflect the behavior patterns and interests of another. What is needed is a careful understanding of the public served (the social mandate) and an appreciation of the many social, economic, and political changes that are affecting our institutions and communities. For example, the aging of America is a reality and must be accommodated in program content and approach. But the increasing median age of the population does not negate the fact that there are still children to be served and that the public generally expects its recreation systems to provide (non-self-supporting) programs for the young.

Local agencies must make individual decisions about program philosophy and direction. New roles and approaches must be assumed, but acceptance of the new does not preclude continuation of the old. The configuration of services, approaches, and roles is strictly a local matter. What is basic is the commitment of the park and recreation professional to provide high-quality services and programs that create opportunities for the meaningful use of leisure.

In addition to the questions related to the financing of public park and recreation services, there are issues of program focus, content, and expectations. Each of these topics merits some discussion.

Program focus

As noted earlier, children, especially young males, were the traditional target group to be served by local park and recreation systems. Later, this role was expanded to include adults, primarily those interested in sports, and the dependent: elderly and physically disabled persons. Are these the populations to be served in the future? Is the purpose of public recreation services to provide a safety net for those who are not able to purchase their own recreation experiences? Or is it to provide those facilities that are of such magnitude and cost that only the public sector can offer them?

The answers lie in the experience of the profession and the publics to be served. Perhaps the program of the future will include services such as leisure education, leisure counseling, and technical assistance to private groups—industry, private recreation clubs, and other direct providers of leisure services. For example, it is assumed that local park and recreation departments will assist industries with their preretirement educational programs, identifying for potential retirees the problems of time management upon retirement, the leisure resources available in the community, and the need to develop leisure skills prior to retirement. Similarly, private recreation groups may ask public recreation agencies for assistance in training and certifying activity leaders, selecting equipment and construction materials, and promoting programs that are aimed at nonmembers as well as members, e.g., a community bike-a-thon or 10-kilometer run.

The delineation of responsibility of each level of government is another aspect of program focus. Who is to fund those programs that primarily serve minority and disadvantaged populations? Whose responsibility is it to provide and maintain major resource areas or to provide the capital for resource expansion? Taxpayers tend to support primarily those programs and services that have a direct "user identification"; that is, those that they use or in which they participate. Since most segments of the population are neither disadvantaged nor minority, local park and recreation systems might be injured financially if they concentrate on being a safety net and do not offer programs that will be used by those who pay the majority of taxes. If, however, public recreation agencies are to compete with the private sector to serve the "mainstream" public, how should their programs differ from those of the private sector?

Since both are basic public services, most states have assumed education and welfare to be responsibilities of state government. State governments give grants to local communities to provide and maintain education and welfare programs. Should a similar approach be used for parks and recreation? Some states have begun to enact legislation to create statewide recreation and park funds similar to the Land and Water Conservation Fund of the Nixon-Ford-Carter administrations. Which programs, services, and resources are the responsibility of the state? Of the federal government?

Program content

Program content differs from program focus in that it concerns the services and activities of park and recreation systems rather than the groups to be served or the functions to be undertaken. In response to increasing maintenance and liability insurance costs, privatization, and competition with the private sector, many park and recreation departments have begun to limit the scope of their programs. Although safety and cost efficiency are desirable, they create the potential for bland programs and the loss of public support. Nothing will change the public's image of parks and recreation more quickly than for park and recreation agencies to stop offering activities that involve participant risk or to relegate all public accommodations to the private sector. By dissociating itself from the direct provider role, parks and recreation may also dissociate itself from the public relations benefits that come from being the direct provider.

Program expectations

The public's expectation of a local park and recreation system depends on three factors: the public's past experiences, its present wants and interests, and the effects of social change. The influence of the first is obvious: It is difficult for local park and recreation systems to assume roles that are unfamiliar to the public. If the public expects the local park and recreation agency to be a direct provider, then the agency is somewhat handicapped if it wishes to adopt another role, say that of facilitator or technical assistant, even though such a role would be consistent with the public's current desire to be more in control of its recreation activities and organizations. But the role of facilitator—that is, one who *enables* others to accomplish their goals rather than provide activities and programs *for* them, is somewhat alien both to the park and recreation system and to the public it serves.

Park and recreation professionals have been trained to be leaders, administrators, and managers—not community developers, counselors, and leisure educators. Abandoning the traditional philosophy of providing services without charging a fee and designing the system to be self-supporting is as difficult as changing from direct provision of services to the facilitation of services.

There is some indication that the present wishes of the public—particularly adults—do suggest a new role for park and recreation agencies. A facilitating role may be appropriate if it is phased in gradually or expanded while the more traditional role of direct provider is maintained. The issue may be one of marketing, of modifying the public's stereotype of parks and recreation. But it is also a professional issue. It is dangerous to build program services and administrative approaches to service delivery in response to what may be a passing trend. We need only recall the hula hoop, CB radios, and video games to appreciate the faddishness of public wants. It is safer to rely on experiences than on wants as indicators of program direction. Beware of those who would too quickly embrace entrepreneurial strategies as the answer to current fiscal difficulties or who would redesign our programs of professional education according to the educational and public policy statements of one presidential administration.

Social change overrides both wants and experiences as a determinant of service. Our populations are changing, as are our technologies and attitudes. America has become a society of adults. The median age in 1986 was thirty-four, with one out of nine Americans sixty-five or older. At the turn of this century, the average worker spent 3% of his or her lifetime in retirement; today, 20% of one's lifetime is spent in that life stage. Technological advances have given us new freedoms—such as the video cassette recorder, which enables us to tape our favorite television show while we engage in some other leisure pursuit. We are becoming masters of our own schedules. Technology has also created new patterns of work—flextime, job sharing, and home industries. These changes, coupled with growing political and social conservatism and a desire to be more in control of our destiny, have important consequences for recreation and leisure services.

Conclusion

It is well to say that public recreation serves all, but in reality, particular segments of the population are more likely than others to use public facilities. Each segment may require a different approach, sometimes for the same activity and service. Or, all may expect the same approach. Some groups may want the local recreation agency simply to provide facilities and technical assistance, while others expect the agency to give instruction, supervision, and direction. Each local system must decide for itself to what extent it will play the role of facilitator; offer technical assistance and grants to private recreation associations; encourage and rely upon the private sector to provide quasi-public services; provide leisure education and leisure counseling; implement entrepreneurial strategies; or support particular positions on a range of social and public policy issues.

The challenge to local governmental recreation and park systems is enormous. Not since the beginning of the industrial revolution have so many major forces affected our patterns of work, our views of government, and the values that undergird society. Never have public officials had to deal with such a diverse population and set of interest groups. Never in our history have the opportunities been so numerous. And, never in our history has our future been so dependent on the course of action we are now taking. It is essential, therefore, that we involve in our decision making those we serve or those we want to serve. This should be done at both the macro and micro levels; that is, the community at large should be involved in decisions that affect the overall patterns of services, but each interest group and neighborhood must also have a say in the content and delivery of services. Once the larger parameters of policy have been established, flexibility is the key. We are in an era of change, an era in which leisure is becoming more acceptable and accessible. The future of parks and recreation has never been brighter—or more uncertain. Understanding our history and our mandate will help to determine what the future will be.